Delicious Vegan Italian Recipes for the Whole Family

Kendrick .R Mcarthur

Delicious Vegan Italian Recipes for the Whole Family :
Wholesome Italian Vegan Cuisine to Delight Your Palate

<u>Funny helpful tips:</u>

Invest in quality marketing; it drives brand awareness and sales.

Your essence is a blend of experiences; cherish each one, knowing they mold your character.

Life advices:

Stay inspired; seek out sources that fuel your passion and drive.

Set clear KPIs (Key Performance Indicators); they provide measurable goals.

Introduction

This book is a delightful cookbook that offers a wide variety of Italian-inspired dishes tailored to meet the dietary preferences of those who follow a gluten-free and vegan lifestyle. Italian cuisine is known for its rich flavors and comforting dishes, and this cookbook successfully brings those elements to the gluten-free and vegan table.

The cookbook features a diverse range of recipes, starting with gluten-free vegan Italian pizza. Pizza is a beloved Italian classic, and this cookbook provides creative and delicious ways to enjoy it without gluten or animal products. From classic Margherita to inventive vegetable-loaded pizzas, there are options to satisfy every pizza craving.

Italian pasta dishes hold a special place in many hearts, and this cookbook delivers with a collection of gluten-free and vegan pasta recipes. Whether it's creamy Alfredo, zesty tomato sauce, or rich pesto, these recipes ensure that those with dietary restrictions can still enjoy the comforting and hearty flavors of Italian pasta dishes.

Vegan lasagnas are another highlight of this cookbook. Lasagna is a comforting and filling Italian dish, and the recipes provided here offer gluten-free and vegan versions that are just as satisfying. From traditional vegetable lasagnas to unique spins on the classic, these recipes showcase the versatility of vegan ingredients.

For those who crave the warmth and aroma of freshly baked bread, the section on gluten-free vegan Italian bread is a treasure trove. From rustic Italian bread to flavorful garlic breadsticks, these recipes ensure that everyone can savor the joy of freshly baked gluten-free and vegan bread.

No Italian meal is complete without dessert, and this cookbook doesn't disappoint with its gluten-free vegan Italian desserts. From creamy tiramisu to delicate almond biscotti, these recipes allow individuals with dietary restrictions to indulge in the sweet side of Italian cuisine.

In summary, this is a cookbook that caters to the specific dietary needs of those who follow a gluten-free and vegan lifestyle while celebrating the rich and comforting flavors of Italian cuisine. With a wide range of recipes for pizza, pasta, lasagna, bread, and desserts, this cookbook proves that delicious Italian dishes can be enjoyed by everyone, regardless of their dietary choices. It's a valuable resource for individuals looking to explore the world of gluten-free and vegan Italian cooking.

Contents

Chapter 1: Gluten Free Vegan Italian Pizza...1

Chapter 2: Gluten Free Vegan Italian Pasta 77

Chapter 3: Vegan Lasagnas 155

Chapter 4: Gluten Free Vegan Italian Bread 178

Chapter 5: Gluten Free Vegan Italian Desserts...236

Chapter 1: Gluten Free Vegan Italian Pizza

In the last few years, pizza has become one of the most enjoyed foods worldwide for a reason. The truth is that pizza is easy to make even at home; it's not time consuming and, most of all, it is delicious and versatile as you can start with a base and add any toppings you want. There are literally no limits for it.

But increasing numbers of people are discovering that they suffer from gluten allergies, so they start to look around for healthy alternatives to their usual pizza. This chapter compiles some of the most delicious gluten free and vegan pizzas out there. They are all fail-proof, easy to make and simply delicious and fragrant. Making pizza at home to suit your taste and diet has never been easier than it will be after reading this chapter.

Moroccan Pizza

Moroccan pizza is all about flavors. The spices used are very fragrant, but none of them overpower the other ones. The final taste is well balanced and the pizza is delicious and a little spicy.

Servings: 4-8 slices

Ingredients:
1 gluten-free pizza crust
2 tablespoons tomato paste
1/2 teaspoons Harissa paste
2 tablespoons tahini paste
2 garlic cloves, minced
1 small eggplant, finely sliced
2 small tomatoes, finely sliced
1 small zucchini, finely sliced
2 tablespoons caraway seeds
2 tablespoons olive oil
Salt, pepper
Fresh basil leaves

Directions:

1. Place the pizza crust onto a baking tray lined with parchment paper. Set aside.

2. In a small bowl, mix the tomato paste with Harissa paste, tahini and garlic. Spread this mixture over the pizza crust. Arrange the eggplant, tomato and zucchini slices over the sauce then drizzle olive oil and sprinkle the basil leaves and the caraway seeds, as well as a pinch of salt and freshly ground pepper to taste.

3. Bake in a preheated oven at 375F for 20-25 minutes until the edges are golden brown and crisp and the vegetables are soft.

4. Cut into slices and serve immediately, while still warm, although it's just as tasty when chilled.

Tofu Pizza Margherita

Pizza Margherita is a classic, but if you are a vegan and have an allergy to gluten, you can try this version which uses a gluten-free crust, topped with fresh tomatoes, green onion and basil.

Servings: 4-8 slices

Ingredients:

Crust:
1 cup brown rice flour
1 cup white rice flour
1 cup tapioca flour
1 1/2 teaspoons instant yeast
1/2 teaspoon gluten free baking powder
1/2 teaspoon salt
1 1/2 cups warm water

Topping:
2 large tomatoes, sliced
2/3 cup tofu cream cheese
1/2 teaspoon oregano
2 tablespoons olive oil
1/5 green onion
Salt, pepper
Basil leaves

Directions:

1. To make the crust: In a bowl, mix the flours, salt and gluten free baking powder. Mix the warm water with the instant yeast and let it bloom for 5 minutes. Pour the water into the bowl over the flour and mix well. Knead for at least 5 minutes, adding more flour if the dough is too sticky. Mix in the olive oil then cover the bowl with plastic wrap and set aside to rise, at room temperature.

2. When the dough has risen, flour your working surface well. Roll out the dough using a rolling pin. From this quantity, you can make 2 pizzas. Transfer the pizzas onto a baking tray lined with parchment paper.

3. In a small bowl, mix the tofu cream cheese with salt, pepper and oregano then spread it over the pizza dough. Top with tomatoes, finely chopped green onions and basil leaves.

4. Drizzle olive oil then bake in a preheated oven at 375F for 15-25 minutes, depending on your oven.

5. Serve warm, cut into slices.

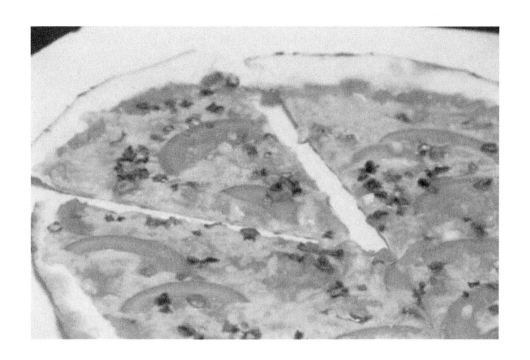

Red Bell Pepper Pizza

Pizza is one of the most enjoyed foods worldwide, but keep in mind that there are also healthy versions of it, such as this red bell pepper pizza.

Servings: 4-8slices

Ingredients:

Pizza crust:
1 cup brown rice flour
1 cup white rice flour
1 cup tapioca flour
1/2 teaspoon salt
1 teaspoon gluten free baking powder
2 teaspoons instant yeast
1 1/2 cups warm water
2 tablespoons olive oil

Topping:
3 red bell peppers, cored and sliced
1/4 cup basil leaves
1/2 cup tomato sauce
1/2 cup tofu, crumbled
1/2 teaspoon dried oregano
Salt, pepper

Directions:

1. To make the crust: In a bowl, mix the flours, salt and gluten free baking powder. Mix the warm water with the instant yeast and let it bloom for 5 minutes. Pour the water into the bowl over the flour and mix well. Knead for a few minutes, adding more flour if it's too sticky. Mix in the olive oil then cover the bowl with plastic wrap and set aside to rise.

2. To finish the pizza: When the dough has risen, flour your working surface well. Roll out the dough using a rolling pin. From this quantity, you can make 2 pizzas. Transfer the pizzas onto a baking tray lined with parchment paper.

3. Spread the tomato sauce over the dough, then top with bell peppers, tofu, basil leaves and a sprinkle of dried oregano, salt and freshly ground pepper. Bake in a preheated oven at 400F for 20-25 minutes or until slightly golden brown on the edge.

Eggplant Pizza

Rich and moist, this pizza makes a great lunch or dinner. It is gluten-free and vegan so it's as healthy as it can be, but still tastes delicious.

Servings: 4-8 slices

Ingredients:

Crust:
2 cups tapioca flour
1 cup rice flour
1 1/2 teaspoon instant yeast
1 cup warm water
1/2 cup coconut milk
1/2 teaspoon salt
1/4 teaspoon dried oregano
4 tablespoons olive oil

Topping:
2 small eggplants, peeled and sliced
2 tablespoons olive oil
1 tomato, sliced
3 tablespoons tomato sauce
Salt, pepper

Directions:

1. To make the crust: In a bowl, mix the flours with salt and oregano. Pour in the water, milk and instant yeast. Mix well then add the olive oil. Knead for at least 5 minutes, adding a bit more flour if the dough is too sticky. Cover the bowl with plastic wrap and let it rise on the countertop, at room temperature, for 1 hour.

2. Once risen, flour your working surface well and spread 2 round pizzas. You can roll the dough as thin or thick as you wish. Transfer the dough onto a baking tray lined with parchment paper.

3. Spread the tomato sauce over the dough then top it with the eggplant and tomato slices, then drizzle the olive oil and sprinkle a pinch of salt and pepper.

4. Bake in a preheated oven at 400F for 15-20 minutes

Polenta Mushroom Pizza

Having a polenta crust, this pizza is moist and delicious and, although you may not think of it that way, just having a bite of it will prove it so.

Servings: 4-8 slices

Ingredients:

Polenta crust:
1 cup coarse cornmeal
3 cups water
2 tablespoons olive oil
1 pinch of salt

Topping:
2/3 cup tofu cream cheese
2 cups mushrooms
1 red onion, sliced
2 tablespoons tomato sauce

Directions:

1. Pour the water and salt into a medium size saucepan and bring to a boil. When it starts to boil, gradually stir in the cornmeal, mixing with a whisk.

2. Let it come to a boil again and simmer over a medium flame, whisking from time to time.

3. When all the liquids have been absorbed, remove from heat and add the olive oil. Let it cool to room temperature then spread 2 round pizzas on a baking tray lined with parchment paper.

4. Spread some tomato sauce over the polenta and top with the tofu cream cheese, red onion rings and mushrooms. bake in a preheated oven at 375F for 20-25 minutes.

Tofu Cream Cheese and Spinach Pizza

Spinach and cream cheese work great together. The final pizza is rich and creamy, while the dough, although gluten-free, is crisp, fluffy and melts in your mouth, making you want bite after bite. It is also healthy and nutritious so it is worth making from time to time.

Servings: 4-8 slices

Ingredients:

Crust:
2 cups gluten-free flour blend
1 teaspoon agave syrup
1 teaspoon gluten free baking powder
1/2 teaspoon salt
1 teaspoon instant yeast
2 tablespoons olive oil
1 cup warm water

Topping:
1 cup tofu cream cheese
1 cup baby spinach leaves
1/2 teaspoon dried basil
Salt, pepper

Directions:

1. In a bowl, mix the water with salt and set aside to bloom for 5 minutes. Stir in the agave syrup, and then incorporate the flour, gluten free baking powder and salt. Mix well with a spoon or a stand mixer and add the olive oil as well. The dough will be sticky. Cover the bowl with plastic wrap and let it rise for 1 hour at room temperature.

2. Flour your working surface well, then spread the dough with your hands so that it looks like an even circle, as thin or thick as you want it. Transfer the dough onto a baking tray lined with parchment paper. In fact, you can roll the dough straight in the pan.

3. In a small bowl, mix the cream cheese with salt, pepper and basil. Spread this mixture over the pizza dough, as evenly as you can. Top with shredded spinach leaves and bake in a preheated oven at 375F for 15-20 minutes.

4. Serve warm, cut into slices.

Broccoli Gluten-Free Pizza

If you like broccoli, this pizza will be a delight baked to perfection on top of a fluffy, crisp, gluten-free pizza crust.

Servings: 4-8 slices

Ingredients:

Crust:
2 cups gluten-free flour blend
2 tablespoons olive oil
1 cup warm water
2 tablespoons coconut milk
1 teaspoon agave syrup
1 teaspoon instant yeast

Topping:
2 cups broccoli florets
1/2 cup tofu cream cheese
1/4 cup tomato sauce
Salt, pepper

Directions:

1. In a bowl, combine the water with coconut milk, agave syrup and yeast. Let it bloom for 5-10 minutes then stir in the flour. Since it's gluten-free dough, it will be sticky and not very easy to work with.

2. Mix in the olive oil then cover the bowl with a plastic wrap and let it rise for 30 minutes.

3. After 30 minutes, carefully spread the dough in a pizza pan lined with parchment paper.

4. Top the dough with cream cheese before spreading the tomato sauce over it and cover with broccoli florets. Season with salt and pepper and then bake in a preheated oven at 375F for 20-25 minutes or until golden brown at the edges.

.Mixed Veggie Pizza

Baked vegetables release their natural sweetness, making this pizza a delight for your taste buds.

Servings: 4-8 slices

Ingredients:

Crust:
1 1/2 cups brown rice flour blend
1 cup warm water
1 teaspoon instant yeast
1 teaspoon agave syrup
1/2 teaspoon salt
1/2 teaspoon gluten free baking powder
2 tablespoons olive oil

Topping:
1 small zucchini, sliced
1 small eggplant, peeled and sliced
1 yellow bell pepper, cored and sliced
1 tomato sliced
1 teaspoon Italian seasoning
Salt, pepper
2 tablespoons olive oil.

Directions:

1. In a bowl, mix the water with salt and set aside to bloom for 5-10 minutes. Add in the agave syrup, then incorporate the flour, gluten free baking powder and salt. Mix well with a spoon or a stand mixer and add the olive oil as well. The dough will be sticky as it has no gluten.

2. Cover the bowl with plastic wrap and let it rise for 1 hour at room temperature.

3. Once the dough has risen, line a pizza pan with baking paper and spread the dough in the pan as evenly as possible. Drizzle with olive oil, sprinkle Italian seasoning then top with zucchini, eggplant, bell pepper and tomato.

4. Bake in a preheated oven at 350F for 30 minutes or until the veggies are tender.

5. Serve warm, cut into slices.

Red Onion Marmalade Pizza

Cooking red onion with vinegar for a longer time, it starts to caramelize resulting in a delicious, savory and spiced marmalade. The crust is thin and crisp, while the topping is creamy and rich.

Servings: 6-8 slices

Ingredients:

Crust:
2 cups brown rice flour
1 cup tapioca flour
1 1/2 teaspoons instant yeast
1/2 teaspoon gluten free baking powder
1/2 teaspoon salt
1/2 teaspoon dried basil
1 1/2 cups warm water

Topping:
1/2 cup tofu cream cheese
3 large red onions
1 tablespoon balsamic vinegar
3 tablespoons olive oil
Salt, pepper

Directions:

1. In a bowl, combine the flours with the gluten free baking powder and salt. Pour in the warm water and instant yeast. Mix well and then add the basil. The dough will be sticky. Cover the bowl with plastic wrap and let it rise at room temperature for 1 hour.

2. Once the dough has risen, spread it into a round pizza pan. Spread the tofu cream cheese and set aside.

3. To make the onion marmalade, heat the olive oil in a medium size saucepan then stir in the red onions. Sauté for 15 minutes until soft and slightly brown. Add the balsamic vinegar then season with salt and pepper. Keep cooking 5 more minutes until fragrant.

4. Spread the marmalade over the dough and cream cheese.

5. Bake in the preheated oven at 350F for 30 minutes, more or less, depending on oven.

Apple, Onion and Tofu Pizza

A sweet and savory pizza, topped with caramelized onions and apples, balanced by a delicious tofu spread.

Servings: 4-8 slices

Ingredients:
1 gluten free pizza crust
2 large onion, sliced
2 apples, cored and sliced
2 tablespoons maple syrup
1 tablespoon olive oil
1 tablespoon balsamic vinegar
2 tablespoons chopped walnuts
1/2 cup crumbled tofu
1/2 cup tofu cream cheese
Salt, pepper

Directions:

1. Put the onion and apple slices in a bowl and stir in the maple syrup and olive oil, as well as balsamic vinegar. Mix well and spread the mixture in a baking tray lined with baking paper. Bake in a preheated oven at 375F for 15 minutes until slightly caramelized.

2. Spread the tofu cream cheese on top of the pizza crust, then cover with the apple and onion mixture.

3. Sprinkle chopped walnuts and tofu and bake in the preheated oven at 375F for 15-25 minutes or until slightly golden brown at the edges.

4. Serve warm, cut into slices.

Spinach and Artichoke White Pizza

White pizza is a classic, but this version is surely much lighter and healthier, while preserving the same creaminess and flavor.

Servings: 4-8 slices

Ingredients:
1 gluten free pizza crust
1 cup spinach leaves, shredded
1 cup canned artichokes, drained and coarsely chopped
2/3 cup tofu cream cheese
1/2 teaspoon Italian seasoning
Salt, pepper

Directions:

1. Mix the cream cheese with salt, pepper and Italian seasoning. Spread this mixture over the pizza crust, then top with spinach and artichoke.

2. Bake in a preheated oven at 400F for 15-20 minutes or until crisp and golden brown on the edges.

3. Cut into slices and serve warm.

Portobello and Kale Pizza

Portobello mushrooms make this pizza really moist and juicy. The final result has a strong earthy flavor, while the kale makes it healthy and nutritious, it being known as fact that kale is packed with iron and fiber.

Servings4-8 slices

Ingredients:
1 gluten free pizza crust
2 Portobello mushrooms, sliced
2 kale leaves, shredded
2/3 cup tofu cream cheese
1/2 teaspoon dried basil
2 tablespoons extra virgin olive oil
Salt, pepper

Directions:

1. In a bowl, mix the tofu cream cheese with dried basil, a pinch of salt and freshly ground pepper.

2. Spread the cream cheese over the crust then top with shredded kale and sliced Portobello mushrooms.

3. Bake in a preheated oven at 400F for 20-25 minutes or until crisp and golden brown at the edges.

4. Serve warm, cut into slices.

Leek and Thyme Pizza

Leek has a similar taste to onion, but much milder and sweeter. Cooked for a longer time, it turns into a creamy, fragrant spread that works great on this pizza.

Servings: 4-8 slices

Ingredients:
1 gluten free pizza crust
2 large leeks, sliced
4 tablespoons olive oil
2 teaspoons fresh thyme, chopped
Salt, pepper
2 tablespoons coconut cream

Directions:

1. Heat the olive oil in a heavy skillet then stir in the leeks. Sauté for 10 minutes until tender. Add the thyme, season with salt and pepper and remove from heat. Let it cool before use.

2. Spread the coconut cream on top of the crust then top with sautéed leeks.

3. Sprinkle with freshly ground pepper and bake in a preheated oven at 375F for 15-20 minutes, depending on your oven. The edges should be crisp and golden brown.

Lentil Crust Pizza with Red Bell Pepper

Gluten-free, dairy-free and light, this pizza redefines the terms *tasty* and *healthy*. So if you like pizza and are a fan of lentils, this pizza is a must try.

Servings: 4-8 slices

Ingredients:

Crust:
1/2 cup uncooked rice
1/4 cup lentils
1/2 cup water
2 garlic cloves
3/4 teaspoon active yeast
1/2 teaspoon salt
1/4 teaspoon gluten free baking powder

Topping:
1/2 cup coconut cream
1 teaspoon hot sauce
2 red bell peppers, cored and sliced
1 cup broccoli florets
Salt, pepper

Directions:

1. Pour 2 cups of water into a bowl then mix in the rice and lentils. Cover with a plastic wrap and let it soak overnight. The next day, drain the water and put the rice and lentils in a blender. Pulse a few times until well blended and smooth. Add the salt, garlic and water and pulse a few more times. Stir in the yeast and gluten free baking powder. Let this mixture rest in a warm place.

2. Line a large baking tray with parchment paper and pour 1/2 cup of mixture into the pan. Being rather liquid, the batter will spread into a circle. Make two such circles on each tray.

3. Bake them in a preheated oven at 400F for 5 minutes.

4. Mix the coconut cream with hot sauce, salt and pepper.

5. Remove the pan from the oven and spread the cream on top of the crust. Add the bell peppers and broccoli and bake for 15 more minutes.

6. Serve warm, cut into slices.

Tofu and Pesto Pizza

Pesto is an aromatic Italian sauce and, although its basil flavors are strong, the sauce itself is not overpowering, especially combined with tofu.

Servings: 4-8 slices

Ingredients:
1 gluten free pizza crust
1/4 cup pesto sauce
1 cup crumbled firm tofu
2 tablespoons extra virgin olive oil
1 tomato, sliced
Salt, pepper

Directions:

1. Spread the pesto sauce over the pizza crust then drizzle the olive oil. Top with crumbled tofu and tomato slices. Add a pinch of salt and freshly ground pepper.

2. Bake in a preheated oven at 400F for 10-15 minutes or until the edges of the pizza are slightly golden brown.

Fresh Corn and Poblano Pizza

Poblano is a mild chili pepper, so the heat in this pizza is not strong, but enough to awaken your senses and make you want one more slice.

Servings: 4-8 slices

Ingredients:
1 gluten free pizza crust
1 poblano pepper
2 tablespoons olive oil
2 cups fresh corn kernels
1 small zucchini, finely sliced, lengthwise
2 garlic cloves, minced
4 tablespoons tofu sour cream
1/4 cup chopped cilantro
Salt, pepper

Directions:

1. In a small bowl, mix the sour cream with the chopped cilantro and garlic, then season with salt and pepper. Spread this mixture over the pizza dough. Drizzle olive oil all over the pizza and top with the zucchini slices.

2. Spread the corn kernels evenly and bake in a preheated oven at 400F for 15-17 minutes, depending on your oven. The final pizza should be crisp and slightly golden brown at the edges.

3. Serve warm, cut into generous slices.

Avocado Cauliflower Pizza

Avocado is a super fruit, being packed with healthy fats. Combined with cauliflower, it turns into a delicious pizza, creamy and moist, mild in taste, but still yummy and enjoyable.

Servings: 4-8 slices

Ingredients:
1 gluten free pizza crust
2 cups cauliflower florets, coarsely chopped
1 ripe avocado, peeled and mashed
2 tablespoons tofu sour cream
1 tablespoon lemon juice
2 tablespoons chopped coriander
Salt, pepper

Directions:

1. Put the avocado, sour cream, lemon juice and coriander in a small blender and pulse until smooth and creamy.

2. Spread this sauce over the pizza crust. Top with cauliflower florets then sprinkle with a pinch of salt and freshly ground pepper.

3. Bake in a preheated oven at 420F for 10 minutes. It doesn't take much time as the cauliflower is naturally tender. The edges should be slightly golden brown and crisp.

4. Serve warm, cut into slices.

Roasted Green Bell Pepper, Kalamata olives and Tofu Pizza

Roasting the green bell peppers only enhances their natural sweetness, while adding a smoky aroma that works great with the tofu.

Servings: 4-8 slices

Ingredients:
1 gluten free pizza crust
2 green bell peppers, roasted and peeled
20 Kalamata olives
2 tablespoons Pesto sauce
3 oz firm tofu, crumbled
2 tablespoons olive oil
Salt, pepper

Directions:

1. Transfer the pizza crust onto a baking tray lined with baking paper. Spread the pesto over the crust. Drizzle with olive oil and top with crumbled tofu.

2. Cut the bell peppers into strips and spread them evenly over the pizza in the pan. Sprinkle a pinch of salt and freshly ground pepper.

3. Bake in a preheated oven at 400F for 10-20 minutes, depending on your oven. The pizza should be golden brown at the edges and crisp.

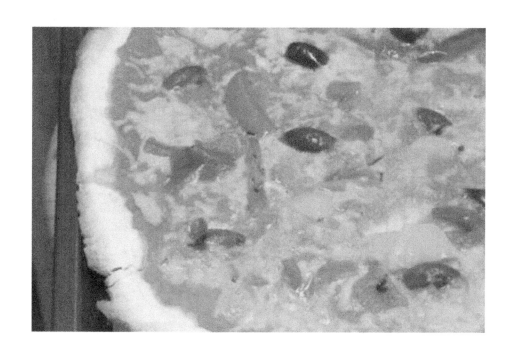

Simple Spinach Pizza

Tomato sauce and spinach are all you will see on this pizza, but this recipe proves that simplicity is always better, as it yields a delicious, flavorful pizza and it is also as healthy as it can be.

Servings: 4-8 slices

Ingredients:
1 gluten-free pizza crust
1/4 cup tomato sauce
1/2 teaspoon dried basil
Salt, pepper
2 cups baby spinach leaves
Lemon wedges for serving

Directions:

1. Mix the tomato sauce with the dried basil, a pinch of salt and pepper. Spread it evenly over the crust then top with spinach.

2. Bake in a preheated oven at 400F for 15 minutes, more or less. How long you bake it depends on your oven. Just check it after 10 minutes. If it looks golden brown at the edges, then it is done.

3. Serve it warm, cut into slices and drizzle with lemon juice if you desire.

Kale, Mushroom, olives and Red Onion Pizza

Kale has almost the same properties as spinach, but it is milder in taste so it can be easily paired with any other ingredients. In this particular recipe, mushrooms, olives and red onion are used to make a delicious, earthy pizza with an incredible taste and fragrance.

Servings: 4-8 slices

Ingredients:
1 gluten free pizza crust
4 oz mushrooms, sliced
20 Kalamata olives
1 red onion, sliced
2 tablespoons olive oil
1 cup shredded kale leaves
1 tablespoon balsamic vinegar
3 oz crumbled firm tofu
2 tablespoons chopped basil leaves
Salt, pepper
2 tablespoons cornmeal

Directions:

1. Preheat your oven at 400F.

2. Sprinkle the cornmeal on a baking tray then put the crust on the pan. Set aside.

3. In another pan, put the mushrooms and red onion, season with salt and pepper, drizzle with olive oil and vinegar and bake in the oven for 10 minutes. Remove from oven and let it cool to room temperature.

4. Top the crust with the mushroom mixture, spread the crumbled tofu and the olives, shredded kale and basil leaves.

5. Bake in the oven for 10-15 minutes until the pizza is golden brown at the edge and the crust is crisp.

Mexican Black Bean Pizza

Mexican means spicy and this pizza makes no exception. However, this pizza is not overly spicy, just enough to awaken your senses. It is also filling and rather creamy and rich, although it only contains vegetables.

Servings: 4-8 slices

Ingredients:
1 gluten free pizza crust
2 tablespoons olive oil
1/2 cup tomato sauce
1/2 green pepper, chopped
1 1/2 cup canned black beans, drained
Juice from 1 lime
1/2 teaspoon cumin powder
1 red onion, cut into rings
2 tablespoons chopped cilantro
Salt, pepper

Directions:

1. Place the pizza crust onto a baking tray lined with parchment paper. Set aside.

2. Put the beans, cumin powder, lime juice and green pepper into a bowl and mash them with a potato masher. It doesn't have to be fine, coarse is better for texture.

3. Spread the tomato sauce over the crust then drizzle with olive oil. Spread the black bean mixture and top with onion rings and chopped cilantro. Sprinkle a pinch of salt and freshly ground pepper.

4. Bake in a preheated oven at 400F for 10-15 minutes, depending on your oven. The edges should be crisp and slightly browned.

5. Serve warm, cut into slices with a dollop of tofu sour cream if you like.

Hawaiian Pizza

The Hawaiian pizza's signature is the pineapple and, although, for some of you, that might sound like a weird combination, the pineapple baked with all the other vegetables turns into a delicious addition to the pizza, making it juicy and flavorful.

Servings: 4-8 slices

Ingredients:
1 gluten-free pizza crust
1 cup fresh pineapple, crushed
1/3 cup tomato sauce
1 small onion, cut into rings
1 teaspoon dried oregano
1/2 teaspoon dried basil
1/8 teaspoon chili flakes
4 oz tofu, cut into thin and small cubes
Salt, pepper

Directions:

1. Place the pizza crust onto a baking tray lined with baking paper. Set aside.

2. Mix the tomato sauce with the dried basil, chili flakes and oregano, as well as a pinch of salt and pepper. Spread the sauce over the

pizza crust. Top with tofu cubes and crushed pineapple, then onion rings.

3. Bake in a preheated oven at 400F for 10-15 minutes or until the edges of the pizza look golden brown and crisp.

4. Serve warm with tomato ketchup or sauce.

Tomato and Sweet Corn Pizza

Tangy, but sweet, this pizza is great to enjoy fresh out of the oven, while the flavors are still bursting out and the aroma is still being released.

Servings: 4-8 slices

Ingredients:
1 gluten free pizza crust
2 ripe tomatoes, slices
1/4 cup tomato sauce
2 tablespoons chopped basil leaves
2/3 cup fresh sweet corn
1/2 cup crumbled firm tofu
1/2 teaspoon salt
1 pinch freshly ground pepper
2 tablespoons pine nuts

Directions:

1. Place the pizza crust onto a baking tray lined with parchment paper.

2. Mix the tomato sauce with the basil, salt and pepper. Spread the sauce over the crust, then top it with crumbled tofu, followed by the tomato slices and sweet corn. Sprinkle the pine nuts.

3. Bake in a preheated oven at 400F for 15-20 minutes or until the edges are golden brown and the vegetables are tender.

4.   Cut into slices and serve right away.

Rosemary and Potato Pizza

Rosemary is a very fragrant aromatic herb; therefore it works great with the potatoes, which have no real distinctive taste. This pizza is rich in flavors and filling, great for your lunches or dinners.

Servings: 4-8 slices

Ingredients:
1 gluten-free pizza crust
1/4 cup tomato sauce
2 golden potatoes, finely sliced
2 teaspoon freshly chopped rosemary
4 tablespoons olive oil
1/4 cup black olives, pitted and coarsely chopped
1/4 cup Cremini mushrooms, sliced
Salt, pepper

Directions:

1. Place the pizza crust onto a baking tray lined with parchment paper. Spread the tomato sauce over the crust.

2. Drizzle with olive oil then arrange the potatoes and sprinkle chopped rosemary. Top with black olives and mushrooms. Sprinkle a pinch of salt and freshly ground pepper then bake in a preheated oven at 375F for 20-25 minutes.

3. Cut into slices and serve warm.

Tempeh Mushroom Pizza

Tempeh is made from whole soy beans and has a different taste and texture than regular tofu. It is high in proteins and fiber so, if you are a following a vegan lifestyle, you should include it in your diet. This particular recipe yields a delicious and nutritious pizza, easy to make at home, with ingredients that any vegan has in his pantry all the time.

Servings: 4-8 slices

Ingredients:
1 gluten-free pizza crust
2 large Portobello mushrooms, sliced
1/2 cup tomato sauce
2 cups tempeh
1/2 teaspoon marjoram
1/2 teaspoon dried oregano
1/2 teaspoon dried basil
2 garlic cloves, minced
1 teaspoon agave syrup
Salt, pepper
4 tablespoons olive oil

Directions:

1. Place the pizza crust onto a baking tray lined with parchment paper. Set the tray aside.

2. In a bowl, mix the tomato sauce with the dried herbs and garlic, as well as agave syrup, salt and a pinch of freshly ground pepper.

3. Spread this sauce over the pizza then top with plenty of tempeh and mushrooms. Drizzle the olive oil and bake the pizza in a preheated oven at 375F for 15-20 minutes or until it is crisp and golden brown at the edges.

4. Cut into slices and serve right away.

Chapter 2: Gluten Free Vegan Italian Pasta

Italian cuisine has always been flavorful and delicious, but with increasing numbers of people having gluten allergies, eating Italian dishes may be difficult. That is, until you get to read this book.

This chapter gathers some of the tastiest Italian pasta dishes that are not only gluten free, but also vegan. They are delicious and fairly easy to make, with ingredients that add not just flavor, but also nutrients, fibers and antioxidants, as well as proteins. Every single recipe is balanced and it can make a great lunch or dinner for your entire family. Although they are gluten free and vegan, the tastes are similar to those you knew before embracing this kind of lifestyle, so you will most surely enjoy all of them.

Potato Alfredo Pasta

Italians love pasta for a reason! Pasta dishes are easy to make and, most of all, delicious and healthy. This particular recipe yields a creamy, rich, Alfredo sauce pasta that is vegan and gluten-free.

Servings: 4-6 dishes

Ingredients:
10 oz gluten free pasta of your choice
10 oz canned cannellini beans, rinsed and drained
2 garlic cloves, minced
2 potatoes, boiled and mashed
1/2 cup coconut milk
1/4 cup soy cream cheese
2 teaspoons nutritional yeast
1/8 teaspoon cayenne pepper
2 tablespoons extra virgin olive oil
Salt, pepper

Directions:

1. Pour a few cups of water into a large pot, add a pinch of salt and bring to a boil. Throw in the pasta and cook until just al dente. Drain and set aside.

2. To make the sauce, put all the ingredients in a blender or food processor and pulse a few times until smooth and creamy. Adjust to taste with salt and pepper then combine the pasta with the sauce.

3. Serve immediately, sprinkled with chopped parsley or coriander.

Pasta Primavera

Fresh and nutritious, this dish gathers lots of vegetables to create a delicious pasta dish. It can also be made ahead in time and refrigerated for a few hours, allowing the flavors to infuse together better.

Servings: 4-6 dishes

Ingredients:
15oz gluten free pasta
1 small zucchini, finely sliced
2 carrots, peeled and finely sliced
1 red bell pepper, cored and sliced
1 teaspoon Italian seasoning
4 tablespoons olive oil
2 garlic cloves, minced
2 tablespoons nutritional yeast
1 1/2 cups cherry tomatoes, halved
2 tablespoons fresh basil leaves
Salt, pepper
Juice from 1/4 lemon

Directions:

1. In a bowl, mix all the vegetables with the garlic, olive oil, salt, pepper and Italian seasoning.

2. Spread the vegetables across a baking tray lined with parchment paper and bake in a preheated oven at 350F for 30-40 minutes until tender. Remove from the oven and put them into a bowl.

3. Pour a few cups of water into a large pot and bring to a boil. Add a pinch of salt and throw in the pasta. Cook until just al dente, then drain and combine with the vegetables in the bowl. Add the basil leaves, chopped, and squeeze a bit of lemon juice before serving.

Sundried Tomato and Basil Pasta

Sundried tomatoes pack all those lovely summer flavors. They are sweet, yet tangy, but they are fresh and their flavors is strong. Combines with basil, they yield a delicious, fragrant pasta that you will love right away.

Servings: 2-4 dishes

Ingredients:
1 cup canned chickpeas, drained
1/4 cup fresh basil
3 oz sundried tomatoes
1 cup spinach leaves
4 tablespoons olive oil
1/2 teaspoon hot sauce
12 oz gluten free Penne pasta
Salt, pepper

Directions:

1. Pour a few cups of water in a large pot. Add a pinch of salt and bring to a boil. When it starts to boil, throw in the pasta and cook until just al dente. Drain and set aside while you make the sauce.

2. To make the sauce, put the basil, spinach, tomatoes, chickpeas and hot sauce in a blender and pulse until smooth. With the blender on, gradually pour in the olive oil. The sauce will be rich, creamy and highly fragrant. Season with salt and pepper to taste.

3. Pour the sauce over the pasta and mix well. Serve immediately.

Vegan Pasta Carbonara

Pasta Carbonara is a classic among the Italian cuisine, but now you can enjoy it in its vegan version. Although the flavors are different, the final experience it's the same as this dish is creamy and rich, delicious in its simplicity.

Servings: 4-6 dishes

Ingredients:
15 oz gluten free pasta of your choice
10 oz tempeh, cut into thin strips
2 tablespoons coconut aminos
1/2 teaspoon smoked paprika
2 garlic cloves, minced
2 tablespoons extra virgin olive
3 tablespoons cashew butter
2 tablespoons tahini paste
1 tablespoon Dijon mustard
1 pinch nutmeg
1 cup soy milk
1/2 cup vegetable broth
1/2 cup frozen peas
2 tablespoons arrowroot starch
Salt, pepper

Directions:

1. Cut the tempeh into thin strips. In a heavy frying pan, mix the coconut aminos, smoked paprika, garlic and olive oil then stir in the tempeh. Cook 10-15 minutes, flipping it once, half way through cooking, to evenly coat it in sauce. It should be crisp and caramelized when it's done—similar to bacon.

2. Pour a few cups of water into a large pot. Add a pinch of salt and bring to a boil. Throw in the pasta and cook until just al dente. Drain and set aside until needed.

3. To make the sauce, combine in a small saucepan the cashew butter, tahini paste, mustard, minced garlic, nutmeg and a pinch of salt and pepper. Slowly pour in the soy milk and broth then put the saucepan over a medium flame.

4. Simmer for 5 minutes then reduce the heat and cook for 10 more minutes. The final result should be thick and creamy.

5. Mix in the pasta, tempeh and frozen peas, cooking on low heat for another 10 minutes. If the sauce becomes dry, pour in additional vegetable broth.

6. Serve the pasta warm.

Peanut Butter Noodles

Savory, creamy and flavorful, these noodles are quick to make, but the flavors are intense and flood your senses with how delicious they are.

Servings: 4-6 dishes

Ingredients:
15 oz rice noodles
2 garlic cloves
1 teaspoon fresh grated ginger
1/2 cup smooth peanut butter
2 tablespoons soy sauce
1/2 cup water
1 teaspoon red wine vinegar
1 teaspoon sugar
1 cup shredded cabbage
4 tablespoons chopped peanuts, toasted
1/2 teaspoon hot sauce
Salt, pepper

Directions:

1. Pour a few cups of water into a large pot. Add a pinch of salt and bring to a boil. Throw in the noodles and cook just until al dente, only for a few minutes. Drain and set aside in a bowl.

2. Put the garlic and ginger, together with the peanut butter, water, soy sauce, vinegar, sugar and hot sauce in a blender. Add a pinch of salt and ground pepper if needed and pulse until smooth.

3. Combine the sauce with the noodles and mix well.

4. Divide them into smaller portions and sprinkle chopped peanuts over each serving.

Creamy Tomato and Basil Pasta

Fresh and fragrant, this pasta dish is great for summer, as a quick lunch. It is light and refreshing enough for those hot summer days. It can also be made in advance as the flavors only get better in time.

Servings: 2-4 dishes

Ingredients;
2 ripe tomatoes, peeled
1/2 cup raw cashews
2 tablespoons water
2 tablespoons olive oil
2 garlic cloves
8 oz gluten free pasta of your choice
Salt, pepper
1/4 cup fresh basil leaves

Directions:

1. Pour a few cups of water into a large pot and add a pinch of salt. Bring to a boil then throw in the pasta and cook until just al dente. Drain and transfer into a bowl. Set aside.

2. To make the sauce, put the cashews, olive oil, garlic, tomatoes, basil, a pinch of salt and freshly ground pepper in a blender. Pulse a few times until well blended and smooth.

3. Combine the pasta with the sauce. Mix well and serve fresh.

Creamy Avocado Pasta

Most of you will know the benefits of avocado, so including it in your diet is a smart move. This particular recipe uses its creaminess to create a rich, delicious pasta sauce, seasoned with plenty of spices to enhance its taste.

Servings: 2-4 dishes

Ingredients:
10 oz gluten free pasta of your choice
Juice from 1/2 lemon
1 ripe avocado, peeled and pitted
2 garlic cloves, minced
1/4 teaspoon dried oregano
2 tablespoons basil leaves
2 tablespoons parsley leaves
2 tablespoons olive oil
Salt, pepper

Directions:

1. Pour a few cups of water into a large pot. Add a pinch of salt and bring to a boil. Add the pasta and cook until just al dente. Drain and set aside in a bowl.

2. To make the sauce, put the avocado, lemon juice, garlic, oregano, basil, parsley and olive oil in a blender and pulse until well blended,

smooth and creamy. Adjust to taste with salt and pepper then pour the sauce over the pasta in the bowl. Mix to evenly coat the pasta.

3.   Serve fresh, right away.

Spinach Pasta

As healthy as spinach is, not all of us like it, but that really depends on how it is being cooked. This particular recipe yields delicious, simply flavored pasta, with a mild taste but outstanding flavor. It is fresh and light, great for those days when you fancy this kind of meal.

Servings: 4-6 dishes

Ingredients:
1/2 pound gluten free pasta of your choice
2 tablespoons olive oil
1/2 teaspoon cumin powder
1 small onion, chopped
1/8 teaspoon chili flakes
2 cups spinach leaves
1 tablespoon lemon juice
Salt, pepper

Directions:

1. Cook the pasta in boiling water until just al dente. Drain and set aside.

2. To make the sauce, heat the olive oil in a heavy skillet.

3. Stir in the pasta and cook until soft and translucent. Mix in the garlic and cumin powder and sauté 1 more minute. Add the spinach, chili flakes and lemon juice and cook for 5 minutes on low heat.

4. Remove from heat and stir in the pasta. Adjust to taste with salt and pepper and serve warm.

Green Pea Pasta

Green peas are sweet and tender and they work great in any combination. This particular dish is creamy and flavorful, simply delicious in its simplicity.

Servings: 2-4 dishes

Ingredients:
15 oz gluten free pasta of your choice
2 tablespoons nutritional yeast flakes
1 tablespoon Dijon mustard
1 teaspoon garlic powder
2 small potatoes, baked and peeled
1 cup soy milk
2 tablespoons extra virgin olive oil
1 teaspoon Cajun seasoning
Salt, pepper
3 cups steamed green peas

Directions:

1. Cook the pasta in a large pot of water until al dente. Drain and set aside in a bowl.

2. To make the sauce, mix the garlic powder with the mustard, yeast flakes, potatoes, soy milk, Cajun seasoning and olive oil in a blender.

Pulse until smooth. Combine the sauce with the cooked pasta then mix in the green peas.

3.   Adjust to taste with salt and pepper and serve immediately.

Basil and Potato Pasta

Who would have thought a green sauce could be so yummy?! For a reason, we all think green is not good, but this sauce will change your opinion. Not only is it creamy, but also highly fragrant and nutritious, as well as filling, great for lunch or breakfast.

Servings: 4 dishes

Ingredients:
1 box gluten free pasta of your choice
1 cup canned cannellini beans, drained
4 garlic cloves
1 sweet onion, chopped
2 potatoes, baked then peeled
1 1/2 cups almond milk
2 tablespoons extra virgin olive oil
1 teaspoon apple cider vinegar
1/8 teaspoon cayenne pepper
2 cups fresh basil
1/2 cup fresh parsley
1/2 cup spinach
1 ripe avocado, peeled and pitted
Juice from 1 lime
Salt, pepper

Directions:

1. Cook the pasta in a pot filled with hot water and a pinch of salt. Cook it until just al dente then drain and set aside in a bowl.

2. To make the pasta sauce, put all the ingredients in a blender or food processor and pulse until smooth and creamy.

3. Adjust the flavor with salt and pepper then combine the sauce with the pasta. Mix well and serve fresh.

Spaghetti Olio e Aglio

This pasta dish is a classic and it's perfect in its simplicity. The pasta only contains a few simple ingredients, but the flavors come together nicely.

Servings: 2-4 dishes

Ingredients:
10 oz gluten free spaghetti
1 teaspoon red chili flakes
2 garlic cloves, minced
2 tablespoons extra virgin olive oil
1 tablespoon chopped fresh parsley
Salt, pepper

Directions:

1. Cook the pasta according to the package instructions, until just al dente. Drain and set aside.

2. In a small frying pan, heat the olive oil then stir in the garlic and chili flakes and cook 1 minute until fragrant. Pour the oil over the pasta and adjust the flavor with salt and pepper.

3. Serve sprinkled with chopped parsley.

Vegetable Noodles

Noodles are very versatile. They can be cooked with any vegetables and they are tender, creamy and flavorful. This recipe uses vegetables for even more flavor.

Servings: 2-4 dishes

Ingredients:
1 package rice noodles
1 cup broccoli florets
1 carrot, peeled and shredded
2 green onions, finely chopped
2 celery stalks, chopped
1/2 cup peanut butter
Juice from 1 orange
4 tablespoons coconut aminos
1/2 teaspoon red chili flakes
1 package firm tofu, cubed
Salt, pepper

Directions:

1. Cook the noodles according to the instructions found on the package. Drain and set aside.

2. In a small bowl, mix the orange juice, peanut butter, coconut aminos, chili flakes and green onions.

3. Put the broccoli, carrot, tofu and celery in a frying pan with 2 tablespoons olive oil and cook until tender, about 10 minutes, on low heat, stirring frequently. Stir in the sauce and cook 5 more minutes then add the noodles.

4. Cook just 2 more minutes and then serve warm, sprinkled with freshly ground pepper if you desire.

Guacamole Pasta

Guacamole is a delicious, creamy dip with Mexican flavors. It works great as pasta sauce as well because the pasta get coated in its creaminess and deliciousness and get infused with its flavors.

Servings: 2-4 dishes

Ingredients:
10 oz gluten free pasta of your choice
2 garlic cloves
Juice from 1 lime
2 tablespoons olive oil
1/2 cup fresh coriander leaves
1 ripe avocado, peeled and pitted
1 tomato, peeled and cubed
1 cup canned corn, drained
Salt, pepper

Directions:

1. Pour a few cups of water into a large pot. Add a pinch of salt and bring to a boil. Throw in the pasta and cook until just al dente. Drain and set aside in a bowl.

2. In a blender, put the garlic, avocado, olive oil, lime juice, coriander, a pinch of salt and pepper. Pulse until creamy and smooth.

3. Fold in the cubed tomato and corn then mix this sauce with the cooked pasta. Adjust to taste with salt and pepper and serve right away.

Arugula Pesto Pasta

Arugula pesto is a bit out of the ordinary, but it is simple to make and it tastes great if you are an arugula fan. It may be bitter compared with the flavors you are used to, but it is very healthy and creamy.

Servings: 2-4 dishes

Ingredients:
10 oz gluten free pasta
1 ripe avocado, peeled and pitted
2 garlic cloves
Juice from 1 lime
2 cups fresh baby arugula
1/2 cup cherry tomatoes, halved
Salt, pepper

Directions:

1. Cook the pasta according to package instructions, until just al dente. Drain and set aside in a bowl.

2. In a blender, mix the avocado with the arugula, lime juice and garlic cloves. Add a pinch of salt and pepper and pulse until creamy.

3. Combine the pasta with the pesto and mix well. Serve right away, topped with cherry tomatoes.

Bok Choy and Black Sesame Pasta

Bok choy is an Asian sort of cabbage, very tender and delicious in its freshness. In this particular recipe, it is being used to create a creamy, incredibly flavorful sauce that works great with the toasted, earthy sesame seeds.

Servings: 4-6 dishes

Ingredients:
15 oz gluten free pasta of your choice
4 small bok choy
1 cup fresh cilantro leaves
4 garlic cloves
1 teaspoon fresh ginger
Juice from 1/2 lemon
1/4 cup extra virgin olive oil
4 tablespoons black sesame seeds
Salt, pepper

Directions:

1. Cook the pasta according to the instructions found on the package. Drain and set aside in a bowl until needed.

2. In a blender or food processor, put the blender, cilantro, garlic, ginger and lemon juice. Pulse until smooth. With the blender running,

gradually pour in the olive oil. Adjust the taste with salt and pepper and combine the pasta with the sauce, in the bowl.

3. Serve on large plates, sprinkled with black sesame seeds, slightly toasted to release flavors.

Kale Pasta

Kale is just as healthy as spinach, if not even more so. It has lots of vitamins, fibers and antioxidants so you should consume it at least a couple of times per month. This particular recipe is easy to make and it doesn't require the kale to be cooked so you can take advantage of their full nutrient content.

Servings: 4-6 dishes

Ingredients:
1 pound gluten free pasta of your choice
1/2 cup finely diced firm tofu
4 kale leaves, stems removed
1/2 cup walnuts
2 tablespoons olive oil
2 tablespoons lemon juice
2 tablespoons fresh parsley
2 tablespoons nutritional yeast flakes
Salt, pepper

Directions:

1. Cook the pasta according to the instructions found on the package. Drain well and set aside in a bowl.

2. Heat the olive oil in a small frying pan and cook the tofu until crisp and golden brown. Set aside.

3. Put the kale, walnuts, lemon juice, parsley and nutritional yeast in a blender and pulse until smooth and creamy. Adjust to taste with salt and freshly ground pepper.

4. Combine the sauce with the pasta and serve topped with crisp tofu.

Grilled Veggie Spaghetti

By grilling the vegetables we release their natural flavors and sweetness so they are tastier and more flavorful. The final result is a delicious pasta dish, nutritious and rich in great aromas.

Servings: 4-6 dishes

Ingredients:

1 small zucchini, finely sliced lengthwise
1 carrot, finely sliced lengthwise
1 red bell pepper
1 small eggplant, peeled and cut into thin strips
1/4 cup extra virgin olive oil
1 tablespoon balsamic vinegar
2 tablespoons sunflower seeds
Salt, pepper
10 oz gluten free pasta of your choice

Directions:

1. Cook the pasta in a large pot of boiling water until just al dente. Drain well and transfer into a bowl. Set aside.

2. Put all the vegetables in a bowl and drizzle them with olive oil. Sprinkle a pinch of salt and pepper then grill each slice on the heated grill pan until tender and slightly golden brown. Remove from pan into the same bowl where there is some olive oil left and pour in the balsamic vinegar.

3. Mix well then add the pasta. Give it a good mix then serve the pasta topped with sunflower seeds.

Tofu Stuffed Shell Pasta

Stuffed pasta is special because underneath the cooked pasta there is a moist, flavorful and creamy layer of filling that floods your mouth with an incredible taste, hard to forget.

Servings: 4-6 dishes

Ingredients:
2 tablespoons olive oil
1 package firm tofu
1/2 cup cashew nuts, soaked over night in water
2 garlic cloves
1 sweet onion
1 cup frozen spinach, thawed and squeezed to remove the liquid
2 tablespoons nutritional yeast
20 jumbo gluten free pasta shells
2 cups tomato sauce
1 teaspoon dried basil
Salt, pepper   \

Directions:

1. Heat the olive oil in a heavy skillet. Sauté the onion and garlic for 2 minutes until soft. Add the spinach and cook 2 more minutes. Remove from heat.

2. Put the tofu in a food processor and add the cashew nuts. Pulse until smooth and creamy. Fold in the onion and spinach mixture. Add

the nutritional yeast. Adjust the taste with salt and pepper.

3.   Cook the pasta shells in boiling water until just al dente.

4.   Fill each shell with the tofu and spinach filling then arrange the pasta in a small deep dish baking pan. Cover with tomato sauce, mixed with dried basil, and cook in a preheated oven at 350F for 20-30 minutes.

5.   Serve them warm.

Wild Mushroom Pasta

Wild mushrooms have an intense taste, but combined with pasta they turn out delicious and they are definitely worth a try if you like earthy flavors.

Servings: 2-4 dishes

Ingredients:
5 oz mixed wild mushrooms, sliced
10 oz gluten free pasta
2 tablespoons olive oil
2 garlic cloves, chopped
2 tablespoons chopped parsley
Salt, pepper

Directions:

1. Cook the pasta in a large pot of boiling water until just al dente. Drain and set aside in a bowl.

2. To make the sauce, simply heat the olive oil in a frying pan. Stir in the mushrooms and sauté for 5-10 minutes then add the garlic and parsley and cook 2 more minutes on low heat. Adjust the taste with salt and pepper.

3. Combine the mushrooms with the pasta and mix well.

4. Serve right away.

Pumpkin Mac and Cheese

If you love Mac and cheese, you can now enjoy it in its vegan form. It is equally creamy and flavorful, so delicious that you won't even tell the difference. Plus, it is much healthier.

Servings: 4-6 dishes

Ingredients:
1 butternut squash
2 tablespoons olive oil
3/4 cup almond milk
1 tablespoon arrowroot powder
1 teaspoon Dijon mustard
6 tablespoons nutritional yeast
1/2 teaspoon garlic powder
1/2 teaspoon onion powder
1 tablespoon lemon juice
Salt, pepper
16 oz gluten free pasta of your choice

Directions:

1. Peel the squash and cut it into cubes. Arrange them all in a deep dish baking pan, drizzle with olive oil and bake in a preheated oven at 400F for 40 minutes or until tender.

2. Add 2 tablespoons of olive oil to a saucepan. Mix the arrowroot with the milk and pour it into the saucepan. Cook on low heat until it starts

to thicken, mixing all the time to prevent it from sticking. Add the garlic powder, onion powder, lemon juice, mustard and nutritional yeast.

3.   Blend the squash and add 2 cups of it into the pot, over the sauce. Remove from heat.

4.   Cook the pasta in a pot of boiling water until just al dente. Drain and put the pasta into the saucepan. Mix well and serve warm.

Tomato Walnut Pasta

Tomatoes are slightly tangy, but combined with walnuts they turn into this delicious, luscious sauce that embraces every piece of pasta, making it incredibly tasty.

.

Servings: 4-6 dishes

Ingredients:
2 cups canned crushed tomatoes
2 tablespoons olive oil
1 small onion, chopped
1 teaspoon dried oregano
1/4 cup basil leaves
1/4 cup nutritional yeast flakes
1 cup fresh spinach
3/4 cup walnuts, toasted and chopped
Salt, pepper
15 oz gluten free pasta of your choice

Directions:

1. Cook the pasta in a large pot of boiling water until just al dente. Drain and set aside in a bowl until needed.

2. In a blender or food processor, combine the walnuts with the spinach and basil. Pulse until smooth and set aside.

3. Heat the olive oil in a heavy pan and sauté the onion for 5 minutes until soft. Add the oregano, tomatoes, salt and pepper and cook for 10 minutes. Stir in the blended walnut mixture and cook another 5 minutes, stirring all the time. Adjust to taste with salt and pepper and add the yeast flakes. Remove from heat and stir in the pasta. Serve immediately.

Tomato and Mushroom Pasta

Cooked for a longer period of time, this sauce turns very creamy and flavorful as the ingredients have enough time to release their aroma properly then they blend together perfectly, creating a delicious pasta dish.

Servings: 4-6 dishes

Ingredients:
15 oz gluten free pasta of your choice
2 tablespoons extra virgin olive oil
1 small onion, chopped
2 garlic cloves, minced
2 cups sliced Cremini mushrooms
2 cups tomato sauce
1/2 cup fresh basil leaves
1/2 cup nutritional yeast flakes
1 teaspoon dried oregano
1/8 teaspoon red chili flakes
Salt, pepper

Directions:

4. Heat the olive oil in a heavy saucepan and stir in the onion. Cook until soft and translucent then add the garlic and mushrooms. Cook for 5-10 minutes then stir in the tomato sauce, dried oregano, chili flakes, salt and freshly ground pepper.

5. Cover with a lid and cook on a low heat for 20-30 minutes. Mix in the yeast flakes and chopped basil then remove from heat.

6. Cook the pasta in a large pot of boiling water until just al dente. Drain it well and stir it into the sauce. Mix well and serve warm.

Cauliflower and Green Olive Pasta

Cauliflower has a mild taste, but combined with the green olives and all the other fresh aromas, it yields an incredibly delicious dish that has all the right ingredients to become a favorite of yours.

Servings: 4-6 dishes

Ingredients:
2 cups cauliflower florets
1/4 cup water or vegetable broth
1/2 cup green olives, chopped
1/2 cup fresh parsley
1/4 cup olive oil
4 garlic cloves, chopped
1 pound gluten free pasta of your choice
1/2 cup toasted almonds, chopped
Salt, pepper

Directions:

1. Cook the cauliflower florets in a pan with the water or vegetable broth. They only have to be tender.

2. Put the green olives and parsley in a food processor. Add the olive oil and pulse until smooth and creamy. Mix the cauliflower with the green olive sauce and garlic then adjust the taste with salt and pepper.

3. Cook the pasta in a large pot of boiling water until just al dente then drain and mix the pasta with the sauce.

4. Serve immediately, topped with toasted almonds.

Pumpkin and Sun-dried Tomato Pasta

This pasta dish is incredibly creamy and juicy, as well as flavorful. It is also very easy to make so you can have a lunch or dinner ready in minutes.

Servings: 4-6 dishes

Ingredients:
15 oz gluten free pasta of your choice
2 tablespoons olive oil
2 cups pumpkin puree
1 tablespoon basil pesto
2 cups vegetable broth
6 sun-dried tomatoes
10 oz kale, stems removed then chopped
Salt, peppe

Directions:

1. Mix the sun-dried tomatoes with the broth and let them soak overnight. Drain them and chop them finely.

2. Cook the pasta in a large pot of boiling water until just al dente. Drain and transfer into a bowl until needed.

3. Heat the olive oil in a large skillet. Add the kale and cook for 5 minutes until soft. Stir in the pumpkin and pesto. Cook for 5 minutes

then adjust the flavor with salt and pepper. Add the chopped tomatoes and the cooked pasta.

4. Keep cooking 2 more minutes then remove from heat and serve warm.

Tofu Marinara Pasta

Marinara is a classic pasta dish, known for its creaminess and tanginess. It is highly flavorful and delicious and you can make the sauce ahead of time and just freeze it then use it when you need it.

Servings: 2-4 dishes

Ingredients:
10 oz gluten free pasta of your choice
3 tomatoes, peeled and chopped
2 tablespoons olive oil
1 small onion, chopped
2 garlic cloves, minced
2 tablespoons tomato paste
2/3 cup tomato juice
5 oz firm tofu, finely diced
1/2 teaspoon dried oregano
1 bay leaf
Salt, pepper
Chopped basil to serv

Directions:

1. Heat the olive oil in a heavy saucepan and stir in the onion. Sauté for 5 minutes until soft and translucent then add the garlic. Cook 30 seconds and stir in the tomato paste, mixing well. After 1 minute, add the chopped tomatoes and tofu, as well as the tomato juice.

2. Stir in the oregano, add the bay leaf and cook on low heat for 30 to 40 minutes, mixing occasionally. When it's done, the sauce should be thick and tasty.

3. Cook the pasta in a large pot of water until just al dente. Drain well then combine the pasta with the tofu sauce.

4. Serve sprinkled with chopped basil.

Chapter 3:

Vegan Lasagnas

Lasagna is a perfect, accommodating dish: It makes a terrific impression without being laborious. Vegan lasagnas are wonderful as main dishes because they are packed with flavor. I know quite a few people who tasted vegan lasagnas and were very surprised to discover that they were made only from natural products.

Eggplant Lasagna

This recipe is suitable for people who love to cook slowly and thoroughly. The slow cooking process allows the pages of the lasagna to slowly absorb the juices of the sauce and the vegetables.

Serving: One medium rectangle pattern

Ingredients
1 package of gluten free lasagna sheets
3 eggplants
3 cloves of chopped garlic
Olive oil
Salt, ground black pepper
Handful of chopped parsley
Tomato sauce:
12 ripe tomatoes
4 cloves of chopped garlic
6 tablespoons of olive oil
Salt, ground black pepper

Preparation:
1. Begin preparation two days before serving.
2. Prepare the eggplant: Slice the eggplant into thin slices and add salt relatively (coarse salt).
3. Set aside to remove fluid for about 15 minutes. Preheat oven to 356F degrees.

Wipe the eggplant slices and place on a pan lined with baking paper. Grease with olive oil, salt and sprinkle with black pepper. Put in the oven for about 30 minutes, until the eggplant is completely soft.

Prepare homemade tomato sauce
1.   Peel tomatoes and blanch them in boiling water for a few seconds.
2.   Peel, cut into small cubes and place in pot. Add garlic, olive oil, salt and pepper and bring to a boil. Cook over low heat for 15-20 minutes.
3.   Grind in a food processor or with a stick blender until sauce is smooth.

Lasagna component
1.   Spread a thin layer of tomato sauce on the bottom of a heat resistant dish. Place a layer of lasagna sheets (uncooked) and cover with a layer of eggplant and sauce. Again, place a layer of lasagna sheets, tomato sauce, steamed spinach and another layer of leaves.
2.   Spread them over tomato sauce and place a layer of eggplant and a layer of lasagna sheets. Finish with a layer of tomato sauce and sprinkle with chopped parsley. Cover the dish with plastic wrap and refrigerate for two days.
3.   Preheat oven to 356F degrees and bake the lasagna for 40 minutes, until the pastry is ready and gold.

Lasagna with cashew cheese

One of the simplest lasagnas to prepare. The cashew cheese adds a wonderful juiciness and it is really hard to tell that this is a vegan lasagna, especially suits small children.

Serving: One medium rectangle pattern

Ingredients:

1 package of gluten free lasagna sheets uncooked
About 4 glasses of quality purchased Italian tomato sauce
2 ripe red tomatoes, sliced thin
Chopped fresh greens - kale or spinach
Olive oil
Ingredients of homemade cashew "cheese":
2 cups cashews soaked in water for 8 to 24 hours
• 3 tablespoons of olive oil
• 3 - 4 tablespoons of lemon
• 1 teaspoon of salt
• 1 teaspoon of garlic powder or fresh garlic clove
• 1/2 cup of basil leaves (optional)
• 1 teaspoon of palm sugar or agave syrup
• 1/4 teaspoon of black pepper

Preparation:
The home made cashew "cheese":
1.   Drain the cashews and place in a liquid food processor.

2. Add 3 tablespoons of olive oil, 3 tablespoons of lemon, teaspoon of salt, a handful of basil, garlic powder and sugar.

3. Process all ingredients on low speed and slowly raise the speed until you get a paste. Add black pepper and taste.If necessary, add a little more olive oil, lemon juice or salt.

The lasagna:

1. Preheat oven to 356 F degrees.

2. Grease the pan with olive oil and place a layer of lasagna leaves, so as to cover the entire bottom.

3. Spread onto the lasagna leaves a layer of the cashew cheese and a layer of chopped green leaves and pour over the tomato sauce in a thin layer to cover the entire pan.

4. Place on top of the layer of sauce, lasagna leaves, cheese layer and another layer of lasagna leaves. Spread the cheese over them and top it with thin slices of tomato. Third layer ingredients - lasagna, cheese and tomato sauce to finish.

5. Cover and bake for about 40 minutes, until the lasagna is baked and is slightly brown.

Zucchini Lasagna

The zucchini and soy milk give this lasagna a delicate flavor. The zucchini can be replaced with eggplant for those who do not like them.

Serving: One medium rectangle pattern

Ingredients:
One package of gluten free lasagna sheets
For the sauce:
3/4 carton of soy milk for cooking (not sweetened)
1/2 teaspoon of ground nutmeg
1/4 teaspoon of black pepper
1/2 teaspoon of salt
3.5 oz tofu
1 Tablespoon of brewer's yeast
400 ml tomato sauce for pasta (home or ready)
4 tablespoons of olive oil or canola
9 oz gluten free wheat flour

Zucchini filling:
  4-5 zucchinis
1 onion
2 tablespoons of canola oil
1/4 teaspoon of salt
1 Pinch of pepper
1 Teaspoon of basil / dried oregano or fresh

Preparation:

Making the sauce:
1.   in a pot without a lid, heat the soy milk and add nutmeg, salt and pepper. After boiling, reduce heat.
2.   Blend the tofu in a food processor (if necessary, you can add a little water) and add to the pot

Add the yeast, beer, tomato sauce and oil. Bring to a boil.
3.   Lower the heat and gradually add the flour, stirring until the texture is smooth and slightly thick. Remove from heat.
4.   Chop the onion and cut the zucchini into little cubes.
5.   Heat oil in a saucepan or large skillet . Saute onion until golden, add the zucchini and spices and cook, uncovered, for about 20 minutes on medium heat (the zucchini excretes a lot of fluid, which is good because lasagna pages need moisture to soften).

Making the lasagna:
1.   Place a layer of lasagna sheets in a greased baking tray, followed by a layer of sauce and a layer of zucchini. Process is repeated twice more (three pages and 3 layers of filling).
2.   Bake in the oven at 392 F degrees about 30-40 minutes until the lasagna is soft (you can check with a knife or toothpick).

Rice leaves & tofu lasagna

Lasagna with rice leaves is great for people who do not want to eat food with gluten. The tofu in the lasagna absorbs all the flavors and gives the dish a thick texture.

Serving: One medium rectangle pattern

Ingredients:

10 rice pages
3 zucchini, sliced into thin slices
3 tomatoes, peeled, sliced into thin slices
1 white onion, sliced into thin slices
4 cloves of garlic, minced
1/2 of a package of spinach, chopped
1 box (9 oz) tomato paste (if desired, can be made with 10 tomatoes, peeled, finely chopped, simmering for about 1/2 an hour on low heat seasoning to taste)
Tofu container (9 oz) soft, grated

Preparation:

1. Fry onion in olive oil until it gets soft, about 10-15 minutes, add the zucchini and fry over low heat until soft. Add the tomatoes and fry until soften. Add the garlic and spinach and fry about 10 minutes. Add the tomato paste. Cook for about 10 minutes.

2. In a rectangular pattern, lay rice paper and place on top the vegetables mixture, and sprinkle a little of tofu cheese. Place the rice

paper and more vegetables and cheese again, until the dish is full.

3.   Place in oven preheated to a temperature of 320 F degrees and bake for about 1/2 an hour.

Spinach lasagna

One of the simplest lasagnas to prepare. The spinach with the tofu makes this dish very healthy. People who love to cook uncomplicated but very tasty dishes will enjoy this lasagna.

Serving: One medium rectangle pattern

Ingredients:

1 package of gluten-free lasagna sheets (uncooked)

1/2 cup of soy chips

3.5 cups of boiling water

2 spoons of onion soup

3 cups of tomato paste

2 teaspoons of sugar

3 tablespoons of crushed garlic

3 large onions

2 trays of frozen spinach (each tray 9 oz)

1/2 teaspoon of salt

1/4 teaspoon of black pepper

Oil for frying

Preparation:

1. Preheat oven to 392 F degrees.
2. Pour the soy chips into a bowl, add the boiling water, soup powder, tomato paste, sugar and 2 tablespoons of crushed garlic, and stir.

3.   Chop the onion and saute half in a deep frying pan until it turns golden.

Add onion mixture from the bowl and stir. Fry for a few minutes.

4.   Fry the remaining onion in a deep pan until its golden brown. Add the spinach and 2 tablespoons of crushed garlic with salt and pepper, stir and fry for a few minutes.

5.   Using a ladle, pour a layer of soy sauce and mash mixture on the bottom of a deep rectangular pan and arrange a layer of lasagna leaves. Pour over the leaves a layer of the spinach mixture and arrange a layer of leaves over the lasagna.

6.   Pour the mixture of the soy and tomato paste over the leaves again, and continue in this order: Layer of soy mixture, layer of leaves, layer of spinach, layer of leaves and so on.

Bake in the oven for about 25 minutes and serve hot.

Raw lasagna

Raw Lasagna (without cooking) is perhaps the healthiest lasagna there is. The benefits of uncooked food are huge! The primary reason is that the food does not lose its vitamins and enzymes, so as to maintain and nourish the body fully and adequately.

Serving: One medium rectangle pattern

Ingredients:
1-3 zucchinis (depending on size)
4-5 red tomatoes
4-5 dried tomatoes soaked in water for at least 20 minutes
1 bunch of basil
1-2 bunch of cilantro (can substitute spinach \ parsley \ chard, etc.)
1-2 handfuls of pine nuts or walnuts
Salt \ pepper \ sweet paprika \ coriander seeds (optional)

Preparation:
1.   Slice the zucchini into thin slices.
2. Prepare salsa from the tomatoes, sun dried tomatoes, walnuts \ pine nuts, basil and seasoning. Filter half the salsa through a fine sieve. Grind the other half with coriander and filter too. (Leftover tomato juice can be used for cooking or seasoning another dish.)

3. Take a medium pattern. Slice the first layer of zucchini and spread a layer of salsa on it, a layer of zucchini, a layer of salsa, etc., until you get a tall and beautiful lasagna. You can play with the layers, alternating the red and green salsa.

Raw Zucchini Lasagna

A delicious, raw lasagna made with zucchini, tomatoes, cashew cheese, pesto and a tasty walnut topping. It may take a while to make, but the final result is a masterpiece.

Servings: 4-6 dishes

Ingredients:
Tomato sauce:
2 ripe tomatoes, peeled and seeded
1 cup sun-dried tomatoes
1 cup agave, pit removed
1 tablespoon lemon juice
1/4 cup olive oil
2 garlic cloves
1 pinch of salt
Spinach pesto:
2 garlic cloves
2 cups spinach leaves
1/4 cup olive oil
1/4 cup pine nuts
1/4 cup walnuts
2 tablespoons lemon juice
1 pinch of salt
Cashew cheese:
1 cup cashews, soaked over night

2 tablespoons lemon juice

2 tablespoons water

2 tablespoons olive oil

1 pinch of salt

Walnut topping:

2 cups walnuts, soaked a few hours in water

1 teaspoon dried thyme

1 pinch of salt

Directions:

1. To make the tomato sauce, simply combine all the ingredients in a blender and pulse until well blended and smooth. Set aside until you finish preparing the rest of the ingredients.

2. To make the spinach pesto, combine the spinach leaves with the garlic, olive oil, pine nuts, walnuts, lemon juice and salt in a blender or food processor and pulse until smooth.

3. To make the cashew cheese, mix all the ingredients together in a blender and pulse a few minutes until smooth and well blended.

4. To make the walnut topping, crush the walnuts and mix them with a pinch of salt and dried thyme.

5. To finish the lasagna, layer in each plate zucchini slices with tomato sauce, cheese, pesto, zucchini again followed by sauce, cheese and pesto then finish with the walnut topping. Serve fresh.

Chapter 4: Gluten Free Vegan Italian Bread

Bread is, for most of us, the essence of a meal and the truth is that bread can be so savory, flavorful and delicious that it is not fair that people suffering from gluten intolerance cannot enjoy it.

This chapter gathers some of the most delicious homemade bread recipes that are not only gluten free, but also vegan and have Italian flavors and roots. They are incredibly good, moist, great for any meal, amazing freshly made and outstanding when toasted. They are much healthier than the gluten version and, although the texture is different, the taste is just as good.

Black Olive Italian Bread

Black olives give this bread a savory, salty and earthy flavor. It smells heavenly freshly baked and it is great next to any meal.

Yields: 1 loaf

Ingredients:
1 cup sorghum flour
1 1/2 cup potato starch
1/2 cup tapioca flour
1 teaspoon salt
1 teaspoon sugar
1 teaspoon xanthan gum
1 1/2 teaspoons instant yeast
2 tablespoons ground flax seeds
4 tablespoons water
1 teaspoon apple cider vinegar
1 cup warm water
2 tablespoons olive oil
1/2 cup black olives, pitted

Directions:

1.   In a small bowl, mix the flax seeds with the 4 tablespoons of water and set aside to soak for 10 minutes.

2. In another bowl, mix the water with the yeast and sugar and let it bloom 5 minutes.

3. In a large bowl, combine the flours with salt and xanthan gum. Pour in the flax seeds, then the yeast mixture and apple vinegar. Mix well with a spoon then knead with your hands for 5 minutes. Add the olive oil and black olives and knead at least 5 more minutes. Use a mixer and the bread attachment if you have one.

4. Cover the bowl with plastic wrap and let it rise for 1 hour in a warm place.

5. Once the dough has risen, transfer it onto a well-floured loaf pan (or lined with parchment paper) and gently shape it with your fingertips or a spatula. The dough is soft so shaping is not difficult.

6. Let it rise one more time for 30 minutes then bake in a preheated oven at 425F for 10 minutes. Lower the heat to 375F and bake 30 more minutes.

7. When baked, let it cool in the pan then slice.

Marjoram and Oregano Bread

Italy is known for its aromatic herbs and Italians do love using them in everything, even in their bread. Indeed, bread gets so much better with the addition of herbs. It is moist and flavorful, amazing for breakfast or lunch.

Yields: 2 loaves

Ingredients:
1 cup sorghum flour
1 cup brown rice flour
1/2 cup tapioca flour
1/2 cup white rice flour
2 teaspoons xanthan gum
1 1/4 teaspoon salt
1 teaspoon dried oregano
1 1/2 teaspoons dried marjoram
1 tablespoon sugar
2 1/2 teaspoons active dry yeast
1 cup warm water
3 tablespoons olive oil
1 teaspoon vinegar
3 tablespoons ground flax seeds
6 tablespoons water

Directions:

1. In a large bowl, mix the flours with the salt, oregano, marjoram and xanthan gum. Set aside.

2. In another bowl, combine the water with the yeast and sugar and let it bloom for 10 minutes.

3. Mix the flax seeds with water and set aside to soak for 10 minutes also.

4. Pour the water and yeast over the flour mixture. Add the flax seeds and mix well. Stir in the olive oil and mix for at least 5 minutes until it comes together nicely. Having no gluten, the dough will be soft and sticky.

5. Line a loaf pan with baking paper and pour the dough into the pan. Let it rise in a warm place for 1 hour then bake in a preheated oven at 375F for 40-50 minutes until golden brown and fragrant.

6. Once done, remove from the pan to a wire rack and chill before slicing.

Multigrain Bread

This kind of bread is highly flavorful and delicious, because of the high content of grains, such as almonds, sorghum and flax meal. It is also very healthy due to the content of vitamins and minerals and packed with fiber.

Yields: 1 loaf

Ingredients:
1 cup millet flour
1 cup tapioca starch
1/2 cup almond meal
1/2 cup amaranth flour
1/4 cup sorghum flour
2 teaspoons xanthan gum
1/4 cup flax meal
1 teaspoon salt
3 tablespoons olive oil
1 teaspoon sugar
1 teaspoon vinegar
1 2/3 cup warm water
2 teaspoons active dry yeast

Directions:

1. In a small bowl, mix the water with the sugar, vinegar and yeast. Let it bloom for 10 minutes.

2. In a bowl, combine together the flours with the xanthan gum, flax meal and salt.

3. Pour in the yeast mixture and mix well with a spoon or mixer. The dough is paste-like, very soft. Add the olive oil and keep mixing for 5 minutes.

4. Line a loaf pan with baking paper then transfer the dough into the pan. Let it rise for 1 hour in a warm place then bake in a preheated oven at 375F for 40 minutes.

5. When done, remove from the oven and let it cool on a wire rack before slicing.

Oregano Flavored Bread

Herb breads are so delicious and flavorful. This particular one has oregano in it, which gives it an incredible aroma when sliced into it, fresh out of the oven.

Yields: 1 loaf

Ingredients:
1 cup sorghum flour

1 cup brown rice flour

1 cup tapioca flour

2 teaspoons xanthan gum

1 teaspoon salt

2 teaspoons dried oregano

1 teaspoon sugar

2 1/2 teaspoons active dry yeast

1 cup warm water

2 tablespoons olive oil

1 teaspoon vinegar

3 tablespoons ground flax seeds

6 tablespoons water

Directions:

1.   In a large bowl, mix the flours with the salt, oregano and xanthan gum. Set aside.

2. In another bowl, combine the water with the yeast and sugar and let it bloom for 10 minutes.

3. Mix the flax seeds with water and set aside to soak for 10 minutes as well.

4. Pour the water over the flour mixture. Add the flax seeds and mix well to combine. Stir in the olive oil and mix for 5 minutes until it comes together nicely.

5. Line a loaf pan with baking paper and pour the dough into the pan. Let it rise in a warm place for 1 hour then bake in a preheated oven at 375F for 40-50 minutes until golden brown and fragrant.

6. Slice when chilled for a proper slicing.

Almond Meal Bread

Having a strong nutty flavor, this bread works great for your morning meals. Toasted and accompanied by a few fresh fruits and syrup, it makes an excellent way to start your day.

Yields: 1 loaf

Ingredients:
1 1/2 cups almond meal
1/2 cup arrowroot powder
1/4 cup flax meal
1 teaspoon salt
1 teaspoon baking soda
1/4 cup applesauce
1/4 cup water
1 teaspoon agave nectar
1 teaspoon apple cider vinegar

Directions:

1. In a bowl, combine the almond meal with the arrowroot and flax meal. Add the salt and gluten free baking powder. Mix in the applesauce, water, agave nectar and vinegar. Give it a good mix then transfer the dough into a loaf pan lined with parchment paper.

2. Bake in a preheated oven at 375F for 40-50 minutes, depending on your oven.

3. When baked, remove from oven onto a wire rack and let it cool before slicing.

Almond and Coconut Flour Bread

Breakfast bread is the best. It is not sweet, but it is flavorful and delicious, perfect for toasting in the morning.

Yields: 1 loaf

Ingredients:
1 1/2 cups almond meal
1/2 cup coconut flour
1/4 cup flax meal
1/2 teaspoon salt
1 teaspoon baking soda
5 tablespoons vegan egg replacer
1/2 cup water
2 tablespoons coconut oil
1 teaspoon sugar
1 teaspoon apple cider vinegar

Directions:

1. In a bowl, mix the almond meal and coconut meal, as well as the flax meal. Add the baking soda, then incorporate the egg replacer, water, sugar and vinegar. Mix well and stir in the coconut oil. Mix until it comes together nicely then transfer into a loaf pan lined with baking paper.

2. Bake in a preheated oven at 375F for 40-50 minutes or until golden brown.

3. When done, remove from the oven and let it cool completely before slicing.

Teff Bread

Teff is an old grain, mostly used in Egypt, but is has a high content of fibers and minerals so it makes a great ingredient for bread, especially if you plan to use it for breakfast.

Yields: 1 loaf

Ingredients:
2 cups teff flour
1/2 cup arrowroot powder
1/2 cup tapioca flour
1 teaspoon xanthan gum
1 teaspoon salt
1 1/2 cups water
2 teaspoons active dry yeast
1 teaspoon sugar
4 tablespoons olive oil
4 tablespoons ground flax seeds

Directions:

1. Mix the water with the sugar, yeast and ground flax seeds. Set aside to bloom for 10 minutes.

2. In another bowl, combine the flours with the salt and xanthan gum. Pour in the liquids and mix well until it comes together. Having no

gluten, the dough will be sticky and soft. Add the olive oil and mix for at least 5 minutes.

3. Cver the bowl with plastic wrap and let it rise for 30 minutes.

4. Line a loaf pan with baking paper and transfer the dough into the pan. Rise 30 more minutes before baking in a preheated oven at 375F for 40-50 minutes.

5. When baked, transfer to a wire rack and let it cool before slicing.

Tofu Bread

Italians love their bread with cheese, but this version using tofu instead is just as moist and delicious.

Yields: 2 loaves

Ingredients:
1 cup brown rice flour
1 cup white rice flour
1 cup tapioca flour
1 cup sweet rice flour
2 teaspoons xanthan gum
1 teaspoon salt
1 teaspoon sugar
2 tablespoons active dry yeast
1 1/2 cups warm water
1 teaspoon vinegar
4 tablespoons extra virgin olive oil
2 tablespoons ground flax seeds mixed with 4 tablespoons water
1/2 cup crumbled tofu

Directions:

1. In a bowl, combine the water, vinegar, sugar and yeast. Mix well and set aside to bloom for 10 minutes.

2.   In another bowl, mix the flours with the salt and xanthan gum. Pour in the flax seeds and yeasted water and mix well. Add the olive oil and crumbled tofu and mix for at least 5 minutes until it comes together nicely. The dough is rather soft and sticky.

3.   Line a baking loaf pan with baking paper and transfer the dough to it. Let it rest at room temperature for 1 hour then bake in a preheated oven at 375F for 50 minutes.

4.   When baked, let it cool on a wire rack then slice and serve.

Fig Bread

Figs work great in this bread, making it moister and giving it so much flavor that you will want another slice, then another. It is also perfect for breakfast, slightly toasted, with jam or simply as it is.

Yields: 2 loaves

Ingredients:
1 cup brown rice flour
1 cup white rice flour
1 cup tapioca flour
1 cup sweet rice flour
1 teaspoon xanthan gum
1 1/2 teaspoons salt
1 teaspoon sugar
2 tablespoons active dry yeast
1 1/2 cups warm water
1 teaspoon vinegar
3 tablespoons extra virgin olive oil
2 tablespoons ground flax seeds mixed with 4 tablespoons water
1 cup ripe figs, chopped

Directions:

1. In a bowl, combine the water, vinegar, sugar and yeast. Mix well and set aside to bloom for 10 minutes.

2. In another bowl, mix the flours with the salt and xanthan gum. Pour in the flax seeds and yeasted water and mix well. Add the olive oil and mix for at least 5 minutes until it comes together nicely. The dough is rather soft and sticky. Gently fold in the chopped figs.

3. Line a baking loaf pan with baking paper and transfer the dough to it. Let it rest at room temperature for 1 hour then bake in a preheated oven at 375F for 50 minutes.

4. When baked, let it cool on a wire rack then slice and serve.

Tomato and Garlic Focaccia

Focaccia is a type of Italian bread topped with different ingredients, from vegetables to fruits. This version is topped with fresh tomato slices, garlic, oregano and olive oil so the end result is moist and flavorful. This bread could pass as a standalone dinner dish as it is so filling.

Yields: 1 focaccia

Ingredients:
1 cup sorghum flour
1 cup potato starch
2/3 cup millet flour
2 teaspoons xanthan gum
1 tablespoon active dry yeast
1 1/2 cups warm water
1 teaspoon salt
1 tablespoon sugar
1/4 cup extra virgin olive oil, divided
1 tablespoon ground flax seeds mixed with 2 tablespoons water
2 garlic cloves
1 tomato, sliced
1 teaspoon oregano

Directions:

1. In a bowl, mix the water with sugar and yeast and set aside to bloom at least 10 minutes.

2. In another bowl, combine the flours with salt and xanthan gum then pour in the liquid. Mix well, incorporating half of the olive oil. Mix for at least 5 minutes until it comes together nicely, then transfer the dough to a large pizza pan, lined with baking paper.

3. Let the dough rise in the pan for 30 minutes.

4. Combine the remaining olive oil with the minced garlic and oregano.

5. When the dough has risen, brush it with the olive oil mix then top it with tomato slices.

6. Bake in a preheated oven at 375F for 40-50 minutes, depending on oven

.

Red Grape Focaccia

Focaccia is very versatile bread. This particular recipe uses red grapes as a topping and it is rather sweet, more like a dessert, but perfect for breakfast or a snack as it is very healthy and fragrant.

Yields: 1 focaccia

Ingredients:
1 1/2 cups almond meal
1/2 cup coconut flour
1/2 cup arrowroot powder
1/4 cup flax meal
1 teaspoon salt
1/2 teaspoon baking soda
1 teaspoon active dry yeast
1/2 cup applesauce
1/4 cup water
1 teaspoon sugar
1 tablespoon agave nectar
1 teaspoon apple cider vinegar

Directions:

1. In a bowl, combine the almond meal with the arrowroot, coconut flour and flax meal. Add the salt and gluten free baking powder. Mix the applesauce, water, sugar, yeast, agave nectar and vinegar. Pour

over the flour in the bowl. Give it a good mix then transfer the dough into a large pizza pan lined with parchment paper.

2. Let the dough rise for 30 minutes then top with the red grapes.

3. Bake in a preheated oven at 375F for 40-50 minutes, depending on your oven.

4. When baked, remove from oven onto a wire rack and let it cool before slicing.

Rosemary Simple Bread

Fragrant and delicious, this bread is perfect for lunch or dinner. The rosemary flavor is mild, but it kicks in with every bite, making you want more, especially if you are a fan of aromatic herbs.

Yields: 2 loaves

Ingredients:
2 1/3 cups warm water
2 tablespoons sugar
3 teaspoons active dry yeast
1/2 cup olive oil
1 cup millet flour
2 cups sorghum flour
1 1/4 cup potato starch
2 tablespoons coconut flour
1 teaspoons xanthan gum
1 teaspoon salt
2 tablespoons fresh chopped rosemary

Directions:

1. In a bowl, combine the water with the sugar and yeast. Let it bloom for 10 minutes.

2. In another bowl, combine the flours with the salt and xanthan gum. Pour in the water and yeast mixture and give it a good mix. Add the

olive oil and rosemary and mix until it comes together, at least 5 minutes.

3. Let it rise in a warm place for 30 minutes.

4. Line a loaf pan with baking paper then transfer the dough into the pan. Let it rise 30 more minutes and then bake in a preheated oven at 375F for 40-50 minutes.

5. Let it cool on a wire rack before slicing.

Simple Homemade Bread

Homemade bread is supposed to be simple to make and very little time consuming, otherwise it wouldn't worth the time, although the taste does not even compare with the store bought one.

Yields: 1 loaf

Ingredients:
5 tablespoons ground flax seeds mixed with 10 tablespoons water
2/3 cup coconut flour
1 1/2 cup almond meal
1 1/2 teaspoon gluten free baking powder
1 teaspoon salt
2 tablespoons olive oil
1/2 cup almond milk

Directions:

1. In a bowl, mix the flours with the gluten free baking powder and salt. Pour in the water mixed with the flax seeds, the almond milk and olive oil. Mix with a spoon or stand mixer for 5 minutes then transfer the dough into a loaf pan lined with baking paper.

2. Bake in the preheated oven at 375F for 40-50 minutes, depending on your oven.

3. Let the bread cool on a wire rack before slicing.

Soda Gluten Free Quick Bread

Quick breads are excellent when you are in a rush and need fast turnaround bread that works well and it is also gluten free, just like this particular recipe which yields delicious, moist bread.

Yields: 1 loaf

Ingredients:
3/4 cup coconut flour
1/4 cup flax meal
1/4 cup arrowroot powder
1 teaspoon baking soda
1 teaspoon gluten free baking powder
1 teaspoon salt
1/4 cup coconut oil
4 tablespoons ground flax seeds mixed with 8 tablespoons water
1/4 cup soy yogurt

Directions:

1. In a bowl, combine the flax seeds and yogurt. Add the salt, then the coconut flour, flax meal, arrowroot powder, baking soda and baking powder. Mix well then incorporate the coconut oil. The dough will be sticky and soft.

2. Transfer into a loaf pan lined with baking paper and bake in a
    preheated oven at 375F for 30-40 minutes, depending on your oven.

3. When baked, transfer to a wire rack and let it cool before slicing.

Buckwheat Brown Bread

Despite its name, buckwheat is gluten free so it's safe to consume even for those who have gluten intolerance. It is also very tasty and makes and excellent bread, combined with other grains.

Yields: 2 loaves

Ingredients:
2 tablespoons ground flax seeds mixed with 4 tablespoons water
1/3 cup coconut oil
2 tablespoons sugar
2 cups warm water
3 teaspoons active dry yeast
1/3 cup apple juice
2 cups potato cornstarch
1/2 cup tapioca flour
1 cup buckwheat flour
1/2 cup teff flour
1 cup flax meal
2 teaspoons xanthan gum
1 teaspoon salt

Directions:

1. In a bowl, mix the flours with the xanthan gum and salt. Set aside.

2. In another bowl, mix the warm water with the yeast, sugar and apple juice. Pour the liquids over the dry ingredients and mix well until it comes together. Add the coconut oil and keep mixing 5 more minutes.

3. Cover the bowl with plastic wrap and let it rise at room temperature for 30 minutes.

4. Line a loaf pan with baking paper then transfer the dough into the pan. It is soft and sticky so don't worry about shaping it that much. Just flatten it with a spatula.

5. Bake in a preheated oven at 350F for 40-50 minutes.

6. Cool on a wire rack then slice.

Basil Bread

This recipe yields very fragrant bread, a perfect accompaniment to your savory meals. It has a very fresh taste and it is moist and healthy, packed with fiber and minerals.

Yields: 2 loaves

Ingredients:
2 cups white rice flour
1 cup tapioca flour
1 cup sweet rice flour
2 teaspoons xanthan gum
1 teaspoons salt
1 tablespoon sugar
2 tablespoons active dry yeast
1 1/2 cups warm water
1 teaspoon vinegar
3 tablespoons extra virgin olive oil
2 tablespoons ground flax seeds mixed with 4 tablespoons water
2 teaspoons dried basil

Directions:

1. In a bowl, mix the water, vinegar, sugar and yeast. Mix well and set aside to bloom for about 10 minutes.

2. In another bowl, combine the flours with the salt, dried basil and xanthan gum. Pour in the flax seeds and yeasted water and mix well. Add the olive oil and mix for 5 minutes until it comes together nicely. Having no gluten, the dough is rather soft and sticky.

3. Line a baking loaf pan with baking paper and transfer the dough to it. Let it rest at room temperature for 1 hour then bake in the preheated oven at 375F for 40-50 minutes.

4. When baked, let it cool on a wire rack then slice and serve.

Rosemary and Red Onion Focaccia

Loaded with flavor and fluffy, this focaccia is amazing at lunch time, drizzled with olive oil and sprinkles with a bit of salt.

Yields: 2 focaccia

Ingredients:
1 cup brown rice flour

1 cup white rice flour

1 cup tapioca flour

1 cup millet flour

2 teaspoons xanthan gum

1 1/2 teaspoon salt

2 teaspoons sugar

2 tablespoons active dry yeast

1 1/2 cups warm water

1 teaspoon vinegar

1/4 cup extra virgin olive oil, divided

2 tablespoons ground flax seeds mixed with 4 tablespoons water

2 tablespoons chopped fresh rosemary

1 large red onion, cut into rings

Directions:

1. In a bowl, combine the water, vinegar, sugar and yeast. Mix well and set aside to bloom for 10 minutes.

2. In another bowl, mix the flours with the salt and xanthan gum. Pour in the flax seeds and yeasted water and mix well. Add the olive oil and mix for at least 5 minutes until it comes together nicely. Since it has no gluten, the dough will be sticky and soft.

3. Line a baking loaf pan with baking paper and transfer the dough to it. Let it rest at room temperature for 1 hour then bake in a preheated oven at 375F for 50 minutes.

4. Cool on a wire rack and only afterwards slice.

Garfava Flour Bread

Garfava flour is a mix of fava bean and garbanzo bean flour and it has different characteristics and taste to the rest of flours, but it tastes great in this bread, making it moist and filling.

Yields: 2 loaves

Ingredients:
1 1/2 cups warm water
2 1/2 teaspoons active dry yeast
5 tablespoons flax seeds mixed with 3/4 cup water
3 tablespoons olive oil
3 tablespoons maple syrup
1 1/2 cups garfava flour
2/3 cup potato starch
1/2 cup tapioca flour
1/2 cup arrowroot flour
1/4 cup almond meal
1 teaspoon xanthan gum
1 teaspoon baking soda
1 teaspoon salt

Directions:

1. Mix the warm water with the sugar and yeast and let it bloom for 10 minutes.

2. In a large bowl, combine the flours with the xanthan gum, baking soda and salt. Pour in the water, then the ground flax seeds. Mix well then incorporate the olive oil. Give it a good mix for a few minutes then cover the bowl with plastic wrap and let it rise for 30 minutes.

3. Line a loaf pan with baking paper and transfer the dough to the pan. Let it rise a second time for 30 minutes then bake in a preheated oven at 350F for 40-50 minutes or more, depending on your oven.

4. When baked, transfer the bread to a wire rack and let it cool completely before slicing.

Chapter 5: Gluten Free Vegan ItalianDesserts

For most of us, no meal is complete without dessert but when you have gluten intolerance things get more complicated as most desserts contain gluten. That is when the recipes presented in this chapter step in—25 gluten free and vegan Italian desserts waiting for you to try them. They are easy to make, but delicious, refreshing and light, great to end any kind of meal on a high note.

Chocolate Panna Cotta

Panna cotta is 100% Italian, but this particular version is vegan and gluten free without sacrificing the incredible taste and creaminess of a panna cotta.

Servings: 2-4 dishes

Ingredients:
3 cups almond milk
1 cup sugar
1/2 cup water
5 tablespoons arrowroot powder
2 cups dairy-free dark chocolate chips

Directions:

1.   In a small bowl, combine the water with the arrowroot powder and mix well. Set aside.

2.   Pour the milk into a saucepan and stir in the sugar. Put the saucepan on medium heat and bring to a boil. Pour in half of the arrowroot mixture and cook until thick, but do not let the liquid boil.

3.   Remove from heat and stir in the chocolate chips. Let it rest for 3 minutes then mix until the chocolate is melted and fully incorporated. Add the remaining arrowroot and put the pan back on heat. Cook until the mixture looks like a thick pudding.

4.   While still hot, pour into serving bowls or glasses and refrigerate for a few hours. Before serving, top with a few fresh fruits, such as strawberries or raspberries.

Lemon Granita

Granitas are very easy to make, but so refreshing and amazing for those hot summer days when all you want is something to cool you off.

Servings: 2-4 dishes

Ingredients:
3 lemons
1/2 cup sugar
3 cups water

Directions:

1. Put the lemon juice and zest in a small saucepan. Add the sugar and bring to a boil on low heat. Simmer 2 minutes then remove from heat and pour in the water.

2. Strain through a fine sieve then pour the mixture into an airtight container and freeze for 2 hours.

3. Remove from heat and mix with a fork to break the ice then freeze 1 more hour, repeating the same process twice more.

Strawberry and Basil Sorbet

Sorbet is very similar to ice cream, but much easier to make. This particular recipe, despite having basil, which is not very common for dessert, is delicious and very refreshing. The basil gives it a unique flavor that you will fall in love with.

Servings: 2-4 dishes

Ingredients:
2 cups strawberries
2 tablespoons basil leaves
1/2 cup sugar
1/2 cup water
1 tablespoon lemon juice

Directions:

1. Pour the sugar and water into a small saucepan and bring to a boil. Simmer on low heat for 5 minutes then remove from heat, add the lemon juice and basil leaves and let it cool. When chilled, remove and discard the basil leaves.

2. Put the strawberries in a blender and add the syrup you made earlier. Pulse until smooth and creamy then transfer the puree into your ice cream maker.

3. Churn according to manufacturer's instructions then store in an airtight container in the freezer or serve right away.

Flourless Chocolate Cake

Chocolate cake is a delicious classic. Moist, creamy, fudgy, this cake is very rich, fitted for a likewise dinner and, although it has no eggs or milk, it is just as delicious as any other chocolate cake.

Servings: 2-4 dishes

Ingredients:
8 oz dark chocolate, chopped
1/2 cup almond butter
3/4 cup sugar
3 tablespoons ground flax seeds mixed with 6 tablespoons water
1/2 cup cocoa powder
1 pinch of salt
1 teaspoon vanilla extract

Directions:

1. Melt the chocolate in the microwave or over a double boiler. Add the almond butter and mix gently until smooth.

2. Add the sugar and mix until melted. Stir in the ground flax seeds then incorporate the cocoa powder, sifted.

3. Pour the batter into a small cake pan lined with baking paper.

4. Bake in the preheated oven at 350F for 25-30 minutes.

5. When ready, let the cake cool in the pan then transfer onto a serving plate and sprinkle with powdered sugar.

Vegan Tiramisu

Tiramisu is a classic Italian dessert known for its creaminess and coffee flavor. It is delicious, light and refreshing, great to end any meal on a high note, no matter how exquisite it might have been.

Servings: 4-6 dishes

Ingredients:
15 oz extra firm tofu
10 oz raw cashews
1/2 cup espresso
4 tablespoons sugar
1 teaspoon lemon juice
1/4 cup raw sugar
1 pinch of salt
1 tablespoon cocoa powder

Directions:

1.   The day before you make the tiramisu, put the tofu in the freezer and soak the cashew nuts in a bowl with just enough water to cover them.

2.   The next day, remove the tofu from the freezer and defrost it in the microwave. Wash the tofu a couple of times, squeezing out its juices, without breaking it.

3. Cut the tofu into thin slices and dry it with paper towels. Arrange the tofu slices on the bottom of a small square pan. Mix the espresso with the 4 tablespoons of sugar and pour it over the tofu. Allow it to marinade for 1 hour.

4. Put the cashew nuts in a food processor with the salt, lemon juice and 1/4 cup raw sugar. Pulse until they turn into a smooth, silky cream.

5. To finish the tiramisu, layer the soaked tofu with cream in serving glasses and top with a sprinkle of cocoa powder.

Almond Biscotti

Italians have a special relationship with desserts. These biscotti may be crisp, but they are great for your morning coffee or as a snack. Fragrant and filling, they can be also coated in chocolate and enjoyed at a fancy party.

Servings: 4-6 biscottis

Ingredients:
1 1/2 cups gluten free flour blend
1 teaspoon gluten free baking powder
1 teaspoon xanthan gum
1/2 teaspoon salt
1/2 cup sugar
2 tablespoons coconut oil
1 cup raw almonds, chopped
2 tablespoons ground flax seeds mixed with 4 tablespoons water
1 pure vanilla extract
1/2 teaspoon almond extract

Directions:

1.   In a large bowl, combine the flour blend with the xanthan gum, baking powder, salt and sugar. Mix in the almonds, then add the ground flax seeds, vanilla and almond extract and mix well, add the coconut oil and mix again.

2. Transfer the dough to a baking tray, lined with baking paper, and shape it into a large roll. Bake it in a preheated oven at 350F for 20 minutes.

3. Remove from the oven, let it cool 10 minutes and slice into 1/2 inch thick slices. Arrange all the slices back on the tray and put it back into the oven for another 10-15 minutes.

4. Store the biscotti in an airtight container.

Cranberry and Pistachio Biscotti

These biscotti are so fragrant and crisp that you will want to make them again and again.

Servings: 2-4 biscottis

Ingredients:
1 cup gluten free flour blend
1/3 cup sugar
1 vanilla extract
1 pinch salt
1 tablespoon ground flax seeds mixed with 2 tablespoons water
3 tablespoons almond butter
1 teaspoon lemon zest
1/4 cup dried cranberries
1/4 cup shelled pistachio, chopped

Directions:

1. In a bowl, combine the flour with the sugar, baking powder and salt. Stir in the butter, softened, then the flax seeds, lemon zest and vanilla extract. Fold in the cranberries and pistachio.

2. Transfer the dough to a baking tray, lined with baking paper, and shape it into a large roll. Bake it in a preheated oven at 350F for 25 minutes.

3. Remove from the oven and let it cool 10 minutes. Slice into 1/2 inch thick slices. Arrange all the slices back on the tray and put them back into the oven for another 10-15 minutes.

4. Store the biscotti in an airtight container until serving.

Gluten Free Amaretti Cookies

Amaretti are almond Italian cookies that are crunchy and fragrant, great for a Sunday afternoon snack. They are also used as a base for other desserts or even liqueurs.

Servings: 6-10 cookies

Ingredients:
15 oz gluten free almond paste
2 tablespoons ground flax seeds mixed with 4 tablespoons water
1/2 cup sugar
1/4 teaspoon almond extract
1/2 cup almonds

Directions:

1. Put the almond paste in a food processor with the sugar and pulse to break the paste. Add the flax seeds and keep processing until the mixture is well combined and comes together. Fold in the whole almonds then shape small balls of dough.

2. Place each cookie on a baking sheet and bake in a preheated oven at 375F for 15-20 minutes. When they are done, turn the oven on and leave them in the oven until it cools down. This will dry them further, making them crunchier.

3. Store in an airtight container until serving.

Vegan Chocolate Truffles

Truffles are the kind of dessert that's easy to make, yet with an exquisite look and taste. They are cream   nd melt in your mouth.

Serving: 8-10 truffles

Ingredients:
3/4 cup coconut milk
12 oz vegan dark chocolate, chopped
1/4 cup cocoa powder
Toasted coconut flakes to decorate

Directions:

1. Pour the coconut milk into a small saucepan and heat to boiling point. Remove from heat and stir in the chocolate. Mix gently with a spatula until the chocolate is melted and the mixture looks smooth. Cover the saucepan with plastic wrap and refrigerate for 2 hours.

2. After 2 hours, take small spoonfuls of the chocolate mixture and form small balls.

3. Dip each ball either in cocoa powder or in coconut flakes and roll them to evenly coat.

4. Serve them right away or store in an airtight container in the refrigerator.

Chocolate and Orange Cioccolatini

Cioccolatini are small chocolate cookies, flavored with all sort of delicacies, such as fruit zest, nuts, dried fruits, coconut or any other ingredients you like. This particular version is very fragrant due to the orange and has some texture due to the addition of pistachio.

Servings: 2-4 dishes

Ingredients:
10 oz vegan dark chocolate, melted
Zest from 2 oranges
1/2 cup pistachio (or more)

Directions:

1. Line a baking tray with parchment paper.

2. Drop spoonfuls of melted chocolate onto the baking paper. The chocolate will spread a bit, creating a cookie. Repeat until you run out of chocolate.

3. Sprinkle orange zest over each cookie and top with chopped pistachio.

4. Refrigerate for at least 1 hour before serving.

Apple Pie Crostata

Crostata is an Italian baked version of a pie, but it is much more rustic and quicker to do. This version is very fragrant and juicy; it literally melts in your mouth, bite after bite.

Servings: 4-6 dishes

Ingredients:

Crust:
1 cup almond meal
1/2 cup coconut flour
1 teaspoon baking soda
1 pinch of salt
2 tablespoons sugar
2 tablespoons ground flax seeds mixed with 4 tablespoons water
1/3 cup coconut oil
1 teaspoon vanilla extract

Filling:
4 apples, peeled and cubed
1 teaspoon cinnamon
1 tablespoon almond meal
2 tablespoons brown sugar
1 tablespoon lemon juice

Directions:

1. To make the crust: Mix the almond meal with the coconut flour, salt, baking soda and sugar. Stir in the coconut oil, flax seeds and vanilla extract and mix well until the dough comes together.

2. Flour your working surface well and divide the dough into 2 portions. Using a rolling pin, roll out the 2 pieces of dough into a circle.

3. To make the filling, mix the apples with the cinnamon, sugar, lemon juice and almond meal in a bowl.

4. Place a few tablespoons of filling in the center of each dough circle then gather the edges of the dough over the filling.

5. Bake in a preheated oven at 350F for 20-30 minutes until slightly golden brown and fragrant.

Nociata

Usually made around Christmas, this dessert only has a few ingredients, but the final result is incredibly delicious and fragrant. It is a real Italian dessert, very rich and packed with flavors.

Servings: 2-4 dishes

Ingredients:
2 cups maple syrup
2 cups shelled walnuts, grounded
1 teaspoon cinnamon
Coconut oil for hands
Baking paper

Directions:

1. Heat the maple syrup in a saucepan then stir in the walnuts and cinnamon, cooking for 10 minutes. Stir all the time to prevent it from sticking to the bottom of the saucepan.

2. When done, pour it over a cold, marbled surface and grease your hands with coconut oil. When the mixture has cooled down a bit take spoonfuls of it and shape each into a small loaf.

3. Arrange each of them on a baking tray lined with baking paper and allow them to set and cool.

4.   Store in an airtight container until serving.

Simple Chocolate Cake

Made with gluten free flour, this cake is delicious and you can't even tell the difference. Not to mention that it is also vegan as it doesn't use any eggs or milk and that makes it healthier.

Servings: 2-4 dishes

Ingredients:
2 cups gluten free flour blend
4 tablespoons cocoa powder
2 teaspoons gluten free baking powder
4 tablespoons vegan egg replacer
1 cup coconut oil
1 cup sugar
1 cup soda water
1 tablespoons apple sauce
1 teaspoon vanilla extract
1 pinch of salt

Directions:

1. In a bowl, combine the flour, cocoa, salt and baking powder.

2. In another bowl, whisk the coconut oil with the sugar, prepared egg replacer, applesauce, vanilla and soda water. Pour this mixture over the flour and mix with a hand mixer for 2 minutes on high speed.

3. Pour the batter into a greased Bundt pan and bake in a preheated oven at 350F for 40-50 minutes.

4. When done, let it cool in the pan then transfer to a serving plate and decorate with powdered sugar.

Panforte

Panforte is a rich Italian fruit cake that works great next to your morning coffee or as a luscious dessert, so versatile it is.

Servings: 4-6 dishes

Ingredients:
10 oz mixed nuts, toasted
1/2 cup vegan dark chocolate, chopped
1/3 cup glace mixed peel, chopped
1/3 cup glace figs, chopped
1/3 cup glace apricots, chopped
1/3 cup rice flour
1 tablespoon cocoa powder
1 teaspoon cinnamon
1 teaspoon mixed spices
2 tablespoons coconut oil
1/2 cup maple syrup
1/2 cup sugar

Directions:

1. In a large bowl, mix the nuts with the chocolate, glace peel and fruits, as well as the cocoa, flour and cinnamon. Set aside.

2. In a small saucepan, combine the maple syrup with the sugar and coconut oil. Cook on medium heat until the mixture looks bubbling

then pour it over the flour and nut mixture. Give it a good mix then spread it in a small round cake pan lined with baking paper.

3.   Bake in a preheated oven at 350F for 30 minutes.

4.   When done, let it cool in the pan then cut into small slices and dust with powdered sugar.

Gluten Free Gingerbread

There is nothing better than gingerbread during winter, close to holiday. All the spices used flood your house with flavors, while the gingerbread is crunchy and delicious, great with a glass of milk or a cup of tea.

Servings: 4-6 dishes

Ingredients:
1 cup sorghum flour
3/4 cup almond meal
1/2 cup potato cornstarch
1 cup brown sugar
1/3 cup cocoa powder
2 teaspoons gluten free baking powder
1 teaspoon baking soda
1 teaspoon xanthan gum
1 teaspoon cinnamon
1 teaspoon ground ginger
1 teaspoon ground cloves
1 pinch of nutmeg
2 tablespoons vegan egg replacer, prepared as stated on the box
1/2 cup molasses
1/4 cup coconut oil
4 tablespoons coconut milk
1 teaspoon vanilla extract
1 pinch of salt

Directions:

1. In a bowl, combine all the dry ingredients together: flours, spices, xanthan gum, baking powder and baking soda.

2. In another bowl, mix together the egg replacer with the molasses, coconut oil, coconut milk, vanilla and salt. Pour this mixture over the dry ingredients and give it a good mix.

3. Line a loaf pan with baking paper then transfer the batter into the pan.

4. Bake in a preheated oven at 350F for 1 hour until fragrant and cooked through.

5. When done, let it cool in the pan then transfer to a wire rack.

Grapefruit and Pomegranate Sorbet

There is nothing better than a few scoops of sorbet during summer, especially when that sorbet is as flavorful and refreshing as this one.

Servings: 2-4 dishes

Ingredients:
1 cup pomegranate juice
Juice from 2 grapefruits
1 teaspoon lemon juice
1 pinch of ground ginger

Directions:

1. Mix all the ingredients into a bowl then pour the liquid into your ice cream maker. Churn according to your machine's instructions.

2. Serve right away or store in an airtight container in the freezer until serving.

Agave Syrup Dough Balls

These donuts are incredibly moist and delicious, very fragrant and fluffy. They represent comfort food at its peak; great for a Sunday afternoon when you want some family time, enjoying something you all like.

Servings: 4-6 dishes

Ingredients:

2 tablespoons ground flax seeds + 6 tablespoons water

3/4 cup soy milk

1/2 cup applesauce

2 tablespoons vegan butter, melted

1 teaspoon vanilla extract

4 cups gluten free flour blend

1 tablespoon sugar

1 teaspoon gluten free baking powder

1 teaspoon cinnamon

1 teaspoon orange zest

2 cups agave syrup

Coconut oil for frying

Directions:

1. In a bowl, mix the ground flax seeds with the water then add the soy milk, applesauce, melted butter, sugar and vanilla. In another bowl,

sift together the flour, baking powder and cinnamon.

2.   Combine the two mixtures and give it a good mix. Knead a few times then gather into a bowl, wrap in plastic wrap and let it sit for 1 hour.

3.   After 1 hour, remove the dough from the plastic wrap and take small pieces of dough. Shape each into a ball and arrange all of them on a baking tray lined with parchment paper.

4.   Heat a large amount of coconut oil in a frying pan and fry the dough balls until golden brown on all sides.

5.   Remove them from the oil onto a large serving plate, stacking them over each other.

6.   Drizzle plenty of agave syrup over them and serve them warm.

Ricciarelli

Ricciarelli are a traditional almond biscuit made in the Tuscan zone of the country. They are flavorful and crunchy, delicious in their simplicity.

Servings: 4-6 dishes

Ingredients:
2 cups almond meal
2 cups powdered sugar
1 teaspoon orange zest
2 tablespoons rice flour
1/2 teaspoon gluten free baking powder
4 tablespoons vegan egg replacer, prepared as stated on the box
1 pinch of salt

Directions:

1.   In a bowl, combine the almond meal with the powdered sugar, orange zest, rice flour, baking powder and salt. Add the egg replacer and mix well. The dough will be firm and heavy.

2.   Shape the dough into a rectangular piece and wrap in plastic wrap. Freeze for at least one hour then cut the dough into small strips, coat in additional powdered sugar and arrange on a baking tray lined with baking paper.

3. Bake in a preheated oven at 350F for 15-20 minutes until golden brown.

Fig and Blackberry Gelato

Gelato is the Italian version of ice cream. This particular recipe is vegan and uses figs and blackberries for an incredible taste. It is highly fragrant and refreshing, creamy and delicious during summer.

Servings: 4-6 dishes

Ingredients:
10 fresh ripe figs
1 tablespoon lemon juice
1 teaspoon lemon zest
2 cups coconut milk
2/3 cup fresh blackberries
1/2 cup sugar

Directions:

1.   Put the blackberries, sugar and lemon juice in a blender and pulse until well blended and smooth. Mix in the coconut milk and lemon zest then pour the mixture into your ice cream maker.

2.   Churn according to your machine's instructions. When it's almost done, add the chopped figs and finish freezing.

3.   Serve right away or store in an airtight container in the freezer until serving.

Stracciatella Ice Cream

Stracciatella is the Italian word for marbled. This particular ice cream recipe is marbled with dark chocolate and it is not only creamy and easy to make, but also has an interesting texture, chunkier due to the chocolate, but just as silky when it melts into your mouth.

Servings: 2-4 dishes

Ingredients:
2 cups coconut milk
1/2 cup cream of coconut
1/2 cup sugar
1 teaspoon vanilla extract
2/3 cup vegan dark chocolate, chopped

Directions:

1. Mix the coconut milk with the cream of coconut and sugar. Add the vanilla and pour the mixture into your ice cream maker.

2. Freeze according to the instructions of your machine. When almost done, stir in the chopped chocolate and finish freezing.

3. Serve immediately or store in an airtight container in the freezer.

Chocolate Sorbet

Although sorbets are usually less creamy and rich than ice creams, this particular recipe yields a delicious, incredibly flavorful sorbet, perfect for a summer day. It has a very exquisite feel and strong flavor so if you are not a chocolate fan, it's better to find another recipe.

Servings: 2-4 dishes

Ingredients:

2 cups water

1 cup sugar

3/4 cup unsweetened cocoa powder

1 pinch of salt

6 oz vegan dark chocolate

1 teaspoon lemon juice

1 teaspoon vanilla extract

Directions:

1. In a small saucepan, mix the water with the sugar and cocoa powder and bring to a boil. Simmer on low heat for 5 minutes then remove from heat and stir in the chocolate.

2. Mix gently until the chocolate is melted then add the lemon juice and vanilla.

3. Let the mixture cool at room temperature then pour it in your ice cream maker. Churn according to your machine's instructions.

4. Serve immediately or store in an airtight container in the freezer until serving.

Red Wine Poached Pears with Amaretti

Poached pears are very exquisite and great to end a rich meal on a high note. They are fragrant and juicy, incredibly soft and flavorful, especially served with crushed amaretti.

Servings: 2-4 dishes

Ingredients:
4 pears
2 cups sweet red wine
1/4 cup sugar
1 cinnamon stick
1 star anise
10 gluten free amaretti cookies

Directions:

1. Peel the pears and cut them in half. Scoop out the seeds.

2. Put the wine, sugar, cinnamon stick and star anise in a saucepan. Add the pears, cover with a lid and bring to a boil.

3. Simmer on low heat for 20-30 minutes until the pears are soft and fragrant.

4. Remove the pears from the wine and keep boiling the wine until it reduces by half.

5. Serve the pears drizzled with wine sauce and topped with crushed amaretti cookies.

Coffee Granita

If you are a coffee lover then you will find this dessert a delight. It is so fragrant, yet so refreshing. It melts in your mouth, flooding your senses with coffee aroma.

Servings: 2-4 dishes

Ingredients:
2 cups espresso
1/2 cup sugar
2 tablespoons Kahlua or other coffee liqueur
1 teaspoon orange zest
1 cup cashew nuts, soaked over night

Directions:

1. Mix all the ingredients in a bowl and pour the mixture into your ice cream maker. Churn according to manufacturer's instructions and serve immediately or store in an airtight container in the freezer.

2. Put the cashew nuts in a food processor and pulse until they turn into a creamy, smooth mixture, similar to whipped cream.

3. Serve the granita in tall glasses, layered with cashew cream.

Strawberries with Balsamic Vinegar

Simple as it is, this dessert is truly unique and its flavors, despite expectations, come together nicely, creating a refreshing dessert, perfect for summer, especially, when strawberries are in season.

Servings: 2-4 dishes

Ingredients:

4 cups strawberries

4 tablespoons maple syrup

2 tablespoons balsamic vinegar

Directions:

1. Combine all the ingredients in a bowl and let them marinade for 1 hour.

2. Mix well before serving.

Peach and Basil Crumble

Italians love basil and they put it in everything, including dessert. But the truth is that there are some fruits, such as peaches, that work well with basil due to their mild taste and delicate flavor.

Servings: 2-4 dishes

Ingredients:
2 pounds peaches, pitted and sliced
2 tablespoons chopped basil
2 tablespoons sugar
2 tablespoons potato starch
1/4 cup almond meal
1/4 cup coconut flour
1/4 cup coconut oil
2 tablespoons sugar

Directions:

1. Cut the peaches into slices and mix them with the chopped basil, sugar and potato starch. Transfer them into a small deep dish baking pan and set aside.

2. Combine the coconut flour with the almond meal, sugar and coconut oil in a bowl. Mix until the dough looks sandy then spread it over the peaches in the pan.

3. Bake at 350F for 30 minutes until the fruits are soft and the top is crunchy and golden brown.

Lemon Polenta Cookies

As weird as 'polenta cookies' may sound, they are truly delicious, very fragrant, crisp and they store great for a long time.

Servings: 2-4 dishes

Ingredients:

1 lemon
1 cup almond butter
1/2 cup sugar
3 tablespoons vegan egg replacer, prepared as stated on the box
2 tablespoons flax meal
1 cup corn meal
1 cup almond meal
1 1/2 teaspoon gluten free baking powder
1/2 cup dried cranberries

Directions:

1. Put the butter, sugar and lemon zest in a bowl and mix until fluffy. Add the egg replacer and mix well. Mix the lemon juice with the flax meal and let it soak for 5 minutes then stir it into the butter mixture.

2. Add the almond flour, corn meal and baking powder and mix well. Fold in the dried cranberries then drop spoonfuls of batter onto your baking trays, lined with baking paper.

3. Bake in a preheated oven at 350F for 15-20 minutes until golden brown at the edges.

4. Store in an airtight container for up to 2 weeks.

Made in United States
Orlando, FL
01 March 2025

59025458R10181